Clementina

Eileen Dunlop

Oxford University Press 1985
Oxford Toronto Melbourne

For Hamish and Pat Dunlop

Oxford University Press, Walton Street, Oxford OX2 6DP

Oxford New York Toronto Kuala Lumpur
Singapore Hong Kong Tokyo Delhi Bombay
Calcutta Madras Karachi Nairobi
Dar es Salaam Cape Town
Melbourne Auckland

and associated companies in

Beirut Berlin Ibadan Mexico City Nicosia

Oxford is a trade mark of Oxford University Press

First published 1985

British Library Cataloguing in Publication Data
Dunlop, Eileen
Clementina.
I.Title
823'.914 [J] PZ7
ISBN 0-19-271503-8

Phototypeset by Tradespools Ltd, Frome, Somerset

Printed by Biddles Ltd, Guildford, Surrey

Contents

Perhaps it was because old friends were coming to stay that Daisy found herself reliving, as if it had all happened yesterday, that time-sharing month of July, far away in Scotland, when she was thirteen years old. For several years afterwards, she had scarcely been able to think about it at all, without a queer red tide rising in front of her eyes, warning her to turn her mind, urgently, to something else. Her mother said you could never recover completely from such an experience, when you were at an impressionable age – and her mother did not know the half of it.

And yet ... for the past three years, at least, Daisy had believed that she had recovered. Living here in Canada, with her young husband, and now, her baby sons, everything was so blessedly different, and she had certainly managed to blot out from the conscious part of her mind disturbing memories of the past. Not until Wendy's letter had come, telling her that Mick had business in Vancouver, and that they would like to spend a week with her, did she realise that the memories were still there underneath, waiting to flood out and drown the sun. She began to sleep badly, and could not concentrate properly during the day.

For with the sharp recollection of the place and the people, all the old, unanswered questions came back too. Could she have done anything to change what had happened? Had Fate really decided the course of events, or would she have to bear through all her life some measure of responsibility? And had she acted rightly, in the end? Daisy had always known that these questions were not only unanswered, but perhaps unanswerable, yet the nagging feeling of guilt remained. For she alone had been aware, for most of the time, that disaster was in the air. Perhaps she might have acted more positively, at least have tried to change things.... But try as she might, as she absent-mindedly spooned egg into a twin, or lay awake while Rodney slept, she could not decide what she might have done. For no one would have believed her, no one who could have helped. It had all seemed then, as it did now, too fantastic for belief. But it had happened, all the same.

Now, in a Canadian city, winter was melting into spring, and Mick and Wendy were coming to stay. Although she loved them both, Daisy did not know whether to be glad or not. But one thing, for the first time, did seem clear. She must force herself to face her memories now, and defeat them, or come to terms with them. Otherwise, for the rest of her life she would be like a person leaning against a bulging door, trying frantically to prevent its bursting open, and spilling the contents of a dark cupboard across the floor.

1

Chalet by the Loch

From the very beginning, everything had gone wrong. There was the weather, for a start. They had left Aberdeen on the first of July, in a brightness of sunshine so sharp that it pained your early-morning eyes, but before they had been an hour on the road, great rolls of raincloud had puffed themselves across the sky. Half an hour later, it had begun to rain.

'We'll soon run out of it again,' said Mrs Graham hopefully.

'Fat chance,' said Bridget crossly.

They did not run out of it. For mile after mile they drove on the motorway, with the windscreen wipers swishing busily, then for more miles among dark green hills, lonely and unwelcoming behind shifting curtains of mist. By the time they arrived at Benalmond, it was late afternoon, and the girls had to rub peep-holes on the steamy windows to see anything outside at all.

There was time to notice a large, ugly, red and white board, fastened to a crumbling, unicorn-crested gate-post, announcing that this was Benalmond Forest Park, First in Scotland for Time-Share Holidays, but that was all. Mrs Graham eased the Volvo, with its bulging roof-rack, through the gate, and they were rocking and bumping slowly up a narrow, muddy drive, between rows of tall black pine trees. Nothing was visible through them except the trunks of other trees, and above, a few wet scraps of sky. Bridget wrote 'hell' on the misty window with her finger, and hastily rubbed it out with her sleeve.

It ought to have been a happy moment, for they had been looking forward to this holiday for months. All through the winter weather, and the exam fever of spring, they had consoled themselves with the thought of four brilliant summer weeks, living in a luxurious chalet in a forest, on the edge of a loch, wearing pretty new clothes, meeting exciting new friends. And now this. It was particularly annoying for Bridget, who had had a lot of trouble persuading her mother to spend an unexpected legacy on four-weeks-a-year-for-ever in a chalet at Benalmond; Mrs Graham would much rather have spent the lot on a visit to her sisters in Australia. Bridget had, of course, got her own way in the end, but not as easily as usual. Now, as the car emerged from the drive into a square courtyard before a large and seemingly derelict building, and began to nose along a sodden track towards a little group of chalets, Daisy noticed that Bridget was wearing her unfair-to-Bridget expression. Not by any means for the last time.

But then the car drew up outside Chalet No 7; Mrs Graham pulled up the hand-brake with a crunch, and said, 'OK, girls. Hoods up, then out, and start carrying.'

It was a relief to get out of the stuffy car into air that was fresh, if wet. Daisy sniffed the forest smell while she waited for Mrs Graham to open the boot and unrope the roof-rack, then she scuttled to and fro in the rain, staggering under the weight of suitcases, boxes, carrier-bags and baskets. Fortunately, perhaps, she was too busy to notice that for every one load that Bridget carried, she was carrying four. Not that it would have surprised her greatly, as it was the usual division of labour between them. Bridget did manage to put the kettle on, and unearth some slightly squashed cream buns from a food hamper; when the tea was on the table, and the weeping forest had been shut out, everything began to look, and feel, a little better.

'It's a nice chalet, isn't it, Dais?' demanded Bridget, anxious to have her good taste commended.

'Mmn. Lovely,' agreed Daisy, through a mouthful of cream bun. 'I'm looking forward to seeing upstairs.'

'Come on then,' said Bridget. 'Bring your bun with you. We're not going to be able to go out tonight, so we may as well get unpacked, and settled in.'

It was indeed a beautiful chalet, built in the Scandinavian style with a shingled roof, and a wide verandah overlooking the loch. The fittings – theirs exclusively for a month – were every bit as sumptuous as the article in *The Sunday Times* had suggested, away back in the winter, when Bridget had been trying to find something nice for her mother to spend her legacy on. The kitchen was full of pine cupboards and chic Italian tiling, sunbursts of orange, olive and rust upon red. The sitting-room had a rich, dark carpet and lots of deep armchairs and sofas, as well as a huge television set and a video recorder. The bathroom was the most luxurious Bridget and Daisy had ever seen, and they spent a long time there, taking showers, washing their hair, and pottering about in their new towelling bathrobes. Indeed, between unpacking their clothes, eating a large supper and watching a film, the evening passed very pleasantly, and it was not until they were getting ready for bed in the blue-curtained room which they were to share, that the sight of a third, empty bed reminded Bridget of something which she had managed, for a while, to forget. The weather was not the only uncertain element in this holiday.

'Oh, damn,' she said crossly, turning her duffle bag upside-down, and letting paperbacks, make-up, hair rollers and writing materials fall down in a heap on the carpet. 'I'd quite forgotten. She's coming tomorrow, isn't she? This is the only night we'll have on our own.'

Daisy, who was sitting cross-legged on her bed, in her nightie, writing on a postcard, 'Dear Mum and Dad, I have arrived safely,' looked up at Bridget with uncertain brown eyes. She too would have preferred them to have this holiday – the first she had ever been allowed to spend away from her family – on their own, without the company of an unknown girl from a Children's Home. But she was ashamed of feeling this way, and besides, as a guest herself, she did not feel it was her place to say so.

'We may like her,' she said, in a half-hearted attempt at fairness. 'You never know.'

'Well, I bet we don't,' replied Bridget gloomily, as she scrabbled for her hairbrush in the middle of the floor. 'She won't be like us – can't be, if you think about it. It's too bad of Mother, really. Just because she's afflicted with a social conscience, she shouldn't expect everyone else to suffer too.'

Daisy knew that this was unfair. She liked Mrs Graham, who was cheerful and undemanding, unlike her own anxious parents. And besides, she admired someone who not only had a social conscience, but actually did something to help the people she had a conscience about. But she had become so accustomed to agreeing with Bridget that she did not come to Mrs Graham's defence, beyond saying soothingly, 'Oh, I expect it's because she's a sociologist.'

Bridget found her brush, and began to apply it irritably to her long fair hair.

'Well, honestly,' she said. 'She ought to try to curb her enthusiasm. Or at least try not to involve me so much in her daft schemes. Talk about collecting lame ducks. There's always someone weird squatting in our spare room, and now this. I mean, just because your father's a minister, does he expect you to go around shouting hymns all day?' She paused to give Daisy time to giggle, then went on, 'Anyway, it's embarrassing doing good to people. They don't always like it. If I were this – this – see now, I don't even remember her name.'

'Clementina Rattray,' said Daisy, who knew that Bridget could remember perfectly well.

'For Heaven's sake. What a name. Well, if I were this Clementina Rattray, I'd hate being done good to by people like us. Wouldn't you?'

'Probably. But I expect she's used to it,' replied Daisy, as she slid down under her blue duvet, and adjusted the flower-sprigged pillow under her head. 'However, if she's coming tomorrow, we'll just have to put up with her, won't we?'

'I suppose so,' agreed Bridget ungraciously, as she bounced into bed and snapped off the light. 'But it won't work, I'm telling you.'

Daisy sighed inaudibly in the darkness. She knew that she ought to contradict Bridget, support Mrs Graham, and point out that Clementina Rattray would just be an ordinary girl like themselves. But she had been Bridget's friend for long enough to know that she was only easy to get along with if she was not contradicted. Like Mrs Graham, Daisy liked a quiet life, and had never asked herself whether she was paying too high a price for it.

So now she said nothing, and let the conversation drift into a discussion of school, and boy-friends, in which she had little more to do than make interested noises, from time to time. Eventually they fell asleep, to the steady drip, drip of water from the eaves, and the chuckle of tiny waves breaking on a stony shore.

2
Three's a Crowd

During the night, the wind sprang up. By morning every tree was shaking with fury, and rain was bursting like shrapnel against the window-panes. Another prolonged session in the sea-green and gold bathroom seemed a good way of passing the time, and Bridget and Daisy came late to breakfast, extra clean and smelling exotic. They found Mrs Graham, dressed as usual in denim and cotton ruffles, like a student who had somehow forgotten to grow up, drinking coffee at the kitchen table, and smoking the one cigarette she allowed herself in the day.

Mrs Graham held firmly the opinion that, if you put young people where there was plenty to do, gave them books to read, and left ample food in the refrigerator, you had done your duty by them, and ought then to be free to go about your own business. If you had also provided a television and a video recorder, you had done a great deal more than your duty, and deserved to be thanked, profusely. So, when she saw Bridget and Daisy coming through the kitchen door, smelling strongly of the expensive scent she had treated herself to last time she was in Paris at a conference, she thought nothing of announcing cheerfully, 'Now, listen, you two. I've got to go to Glasgow today, to have lunch with some German students who are doing a sociology course at the University Summer School. I've left you a pie and a jelly – if you want carrots and spuds, you'll have to peel them yourselves, right? Clementina will be arriving at two fifteen – the bus will put her down at the end of the drive, and I've said someone will meet her. That means you. I'll be back about five – if I'm going to be later, I'll phone.'

She gulped down the last of her coffee, and got up from the table, her round, good-tempered face shining with happiness. She was a woman well content with life. Bridget, who had turned scarlet, had to draw breath more than once before her voice came. Then it issued in a wail of anger.

'But Mother, that isn't fair. I mean, she's your responsibility, not ours. You were the one who invited her, and now we're left to cope while you go gallivanting off to Glasgow. It'll be ghastly. What on earth are we going to talk to her about? Oh, you are *mean*.'

Mrs Graham turned in the doorway of the kitchen. She was well used to this kind of outburst from her daughter.

'Don't be silly, dear,' she said calmly. 'Young people are always talking. Have a nice day.'

She departed, and Bridget was left staring at Daisy across the breakfast things.

'I'll make some toast, shall I?' said Daisy hurriedly.

After breakfast, the two girls decided to brave the weather, and explore the park.

'We may as well,' said Bridget, as she struggled into her wellingtons and pulled her red cagoule over her head. 'We haven't much longer to enjoy things on our own, have we? Two's company, three's a crowd.'

Daisy did not feel up to arguing with proverbs, so she fastened the hood of her waterproof, and said, 'We really should get some fresh air while we're on holiday, even if we do catch pneumonia at the same time.'

So they shut the door behind them, and set off,

plodding through the trees, sniffing the sharp smell of pine, laced with the softer, sweeter smell of bracken in the rain. The fresh wind buffeted them merrily as they crunched their way over shale and pebbles along the margin of the little loch, past the crude new landing-stage where small boats and dinghies bobbed unattended at their moorings. It was not boating weather, and there was not another person in sight.

The estate of Benalmond Tower, which was now being developed as a leisure complex and centre for time-sharing holidays, occupied only a tiny corner of a vast forest park, most of which was owned by the Forestry Commission. It was criss-crossed by nature trails, hikers' paths and tracks for pony-trekking. Behind Benalmond Tower, which they had passed yesterday in the rain, this forest stalked thick and wide, covering valleys and hills with a striped mantle of larch and pine, from which, in the distance, reared harsh and stony mountain peaks.

The estate itself, Bridget and Daisy discovered, was far from complete in its transformation into a holiday centre. Indeed, it now seemed that the brochure presented a plan for the future, instead of telling the truth about what had been achieved so far. The ten chalets by the loch, of which theirs was one, made the only completed group. There were others half-built on a hill behind, circling a block of flats which was partly inhabited, judging by curtained windows and bicycles standing in the covered entrance. The swimming-pool and the sauna were complete, as were the games hall and the restaurant, pleasant, flat-roofed buildings screened by the birch and mountain ash which grew everywhere. But all around were notices, *'Shops under construction'*, *'Beware lorries turning'*, *'Next phase opening April'*.

'We'll be grey-haired old grannies before this lot's

finished,' said Bridget indignantly, as they ploughed through mud down a tree-bound path, which emerged without warning on to the gravelled courtyard in front of Benalmond Tower.

Even on a wet day, it darkened the sky, and was the most un-holiday-like place one would ever see in one's life.

'How sinister,' Daisy said.

It was not too strong a word.

The Tower reared up out of the clearing, scowling, smoke-scarred and permanent. No amount of modern rearrangement of its surroundings could ever take from it its air of having been there since old, unhappy, far-off times, or its conviction that it would still be there when all the other tawdry twentieth-century buildings had been swallowed up by the forest once again.

'I'm glad we can't see this from our place,' Daisy went on. 'I bet it's got bats, and owls, and things that go bump in the night. Don't you think so, Bridget?'

Bridget tipped back her head to look up at the sagging, crow-stepped roof, and windows that were like small, short-sighted eyes. Her hood fell off, and she screwed up her face as the rain fell straight down on to it. She was not an imaginative girl, but she could see what Daisy meant.

'They're going to turn it into flats,' she remarked, twitching on her hood again.

'Never,' exclaimed Daisy, horrified.

'Yes. It was in *The Sunday Times*. Four luxury flats in a unique historic setting – or was it six? I quite fancied the idea, but they were going to be so terribly expensive – we couldn't have afforded one even if Aunt Jo had left Mother twice as much money.'

'Well, I'm glad,' said Daisy fervently. 'I wouldn't like to spend a night in there, never mind a month.'

She winced at the thought of it.

'Oh, it'll all look different when it's lived in, I suppose,' said Bridget, losing interest. 'Now, come on. We'd better get on back and put that pie in the oven. We don't want to be late for Miss Clementina's bus – she might tell Mother, and get us into trouble.'

While they stood huddling in the rain, waiting for the bus to come, Bridget and Daisy passed the time by reading the small lettering at the bottom of the red and white notice board, which they had not been able to see properly through the steamy window yesterday. From it they learned much useless information, such as the address in Glasgow of the Development Company in charge of the Benalmond Project, that most weeks in January and February were still available to eager holiday-makers, and that Phase Three of the operation, the conversion of Benalmond Tower into six luxury flats, was due to begin –

'Six months ago. Isn't that typical?' Daisy sighed.

They also learned that, as well as swimming, tennis, squash, golf, sailing and water-skiing, pony-trekking was one of the activities in which one could join.

'I'd like that,' said Bridget. 'We might find out a bit more about it, if the weather ever improves. What do you think, Dais?'

Daisy said she thought it was a good idea, speaking generally, but she had become pessimistic about the weather.

'It can't rain for a month, can it?' asked Bridget, uncertainly.

'It has been known,' said Daisy, darkly.

At twenty-five past two, an old blue bus came lumbering in a casual fashion along the narrow road, its hippopotamus flanks brushing the overhanging branches, and bringing down extra showers of rainwater on to its roof. It wheezed to a halt outside the unicorn gates, the folding doors sighed, and opened, and one passenger got out. Then the doors closed, and the bus crawled on up the road towards Kinlochard.

Bridget and Daisy stared after it in dismay. A long moment passed before it dawned on them that the passenger who had got down might be the one they had come to meet. They turned their eyes on her in disbelief.

It probably isn't a good thing to form in advance a picture of someone you are going to meet, although, to be fair, Bridget had not meant to be snobbish when she said the previous evening that Clementina Rattray would not be like Daisy and herself. She had been thinking of shared interests and acquaintances, rather than appearance. If she had thought about that at all, she would have expected the newcomer to look exactly like themselves, an ordinary thirteen-year-old in an anorak and well-worn jeans. Because she did not, neither Bridget nor Daisy recognised her.

She was wearing a shiny red waterproof, with the collar turned up, and rather smart black boots. She was taller than either of them, and was certainly older, though it would have been hard to say how much. She was also beautiful, in a thin, delicate kind of way, with a clear brown skin and dense dark hair which flopped in loose waves around her face. She stood in the rain like a princess, holding a black nylon travelling-bag and a violin case, regarding Bridget and Daisy gravely with eyes half green and half brown. Her straight black eyebrows were very slightly raised.

It was Daisy who recovered from her astonishment first. She asked, 'Are you Clementina?' and the girl smiled at her briefly, showing good teeth.

'Yes,' she said. 'You must be Bridget.'

'No, I am,' put in Bridget hastily. 'This is my friend, Daisy Bradbrook. Mother's sorry she's not here to meet you –' untrue, but Bridget was a conventional kind of person '– she's had to go to Glasgow today, and she won't be back till five. Shall I carry your bag for you?'

'No, thanks. It isn't heavy.'

Clementina fell into step between them, and they walked through the gate, up the rutted, sludgy drive.

'It isn't very nice weather for the holiday, is it?' asked Daisy, making conversation.

'No.'

'Perhaps it will clear tomorrow.'

'Yes.'

'We haven't heard the forecast. Have you?'

'No.'

There was a pause, then Bridget tried.

'Are you very hungry?'

'No, thank you.'

'We'll have some tea when we get back.'

'I see.'

Bridget wanted to roll her eyes at Daisy, but couldn't, because Clementina was walking in the middle. Sometimes people answer in monosyllables because they are shy, but they could sense that this girl was not shy in the least. It was simply that she was the rare kind of person who is quite at ease without chatter – the most difficult companion in the world, if you are not inclined that way yourself. After a few silent moments, highly embarrassing to Bridget and Daisy, Bridget tried again.

'Have you come all the way from Edinburgh by bus?' she asked politely.

But she would never know. This time, there was no reply at all.

They had come round a curve in the drive, on to the courtyard in front of Benalmond Tower. Suddenly it was before them, black and massive against the grey-green of the pine forest at its back. It was disturbing, to a person who found old, derelict places disturbing; Daisy did, and Bridget did not. But even Daisy thought that Clementina Rattray's reaction was odd. She stopped dead, and stood staring. And went on staring. One could not say that the composure of her straight features altered, but her face paled a little, and it was apparent that something had rattled her. She must have been aware that the other two were regarding her strangely, because Daisy saw her make an effort, and pull herself together.

With an attempt at lightness of tone, she said, 'Well – what a horrid old place. What is it?'

'Benalmond Tower,' said Bridget impatiently. 'They're going to turn it into flats. One fine day. Now, come on. Let's get indoors before we drown. This is absolutely foul.'

Daisy and Clementina obediently hurried after her along the path to the chalets by the loch.

If Clementina was impressed by the luxury which the chalet offered – a reaction which would have pleased Bridget – she gave no sign of it. Quietly she followed the other girls upstairs, nodded briefly when Bridget showed her the bathroom, and allowed herself to be ushered into the big bedroom where the blue walls had turned grey from the reflection of the watery day outside. Only then, as she looked around and saw the three little beds in corners, did a slight expression of annoyance show itself on her face.

'Am I to sleep with you?' she asked, and they knew instantly that she did not want them any more than they wanted her. She, too, considered three a crowd.

Although this was perfectly fair, Bridget and Daisy felt aggrieved. But Bridget, although she was disliking the newcomer more every moment, had long experience of being reasonably civil to unwelcome guests. So she said quite mildly, 'Well, yes, I'm afraid so. There are only two bedrooms, you see, this one, and a tiny one next door, where Mother sleeps. She didn't think you'd mind.'

Clementina did not say that she didn't mind. She said, 'Ah well, I suppose it can't be helped,' and slung her bag on to a chair.

Daisy, who had taken off her anorak and boots, sat down on her bed and watched Clementina in a mixture of admiration of her style, and exasperation with her lack of tact. She could sense Bridget's pique, and her heart sank, because she knew that Bridget's first impression of anyone was always the lasting one; she boasted, indeed, that she never changed her mind. Whether Daisy came to like Clementina or not would matter little if Bridget decided against her; loyalty and a sense of obligation to the Grahams would make Daisy feel she ought to side with Bridget, regardless of her own feelings. At the moment, she had no idea what her own feelings were likely to be, but she would have liked freedom to make up her own mind. If only Clementina would say she liked Bridget's hair-style, or admire her blouse.... Daisy watched Clementina taking off her red coat – she was wearing a striped T-shirt and a denim skirt underneath – and hanging it up in her section of the wardrobe. Then, because the atmosphere was getting on her nerves, she said, 'Do you have a room of your own where you live, Clementina?'

Clementina said that she did. Daisy persevered.

'Are there many children?'

'About twenty. They come and go.'

'Have you lived there for long?'

'Three years.'

'Do you like it?'

Clementina, who had unzipped her bag, and begun to lay her belongings in neat piles on her bed, stopped, turned, and contemplated Daisy, who was looking like an anxious fieldmouse with her short brown hair and shining brown eyes. Then she glanced at Bridget, who was leaning on the window sill, pretending to be absorbed in the non-view of the loch under rain.

'Look,' she said flatly, 'I may as well tell you what I suppose you want to know, then you'll be spared the necessity of getting it out of me by degrees, won't you?' She sat down on her bed, and like someone repeating mechanically a carefully prepared speech, went on, 'My father was a journalist on an Edinburgh newspaper. I lived with him until he died three years ago. I never knew my mother – I don't even know who she was. My father died very suddenly of a heart attack, and because I have no other relative living – at least, that anyone knows about – I was taken into care by the Social Work Department. They found a place for me at Torley Hall, near Musselburgh. I wouldn't exactly choose to live there, obviously, but it's all right. The house-parents are nice, and the inmates are just like any other kids, except that they've got more problems than most. Anyway I'll only be there for another couple of months, because I've won a scholarship to a music school in London. Only they won't take me till I'm sixteen. Now, do you think you'll be able to leave me in peace, or is there anything else you'd like to know?'

Daisy was completely taken aback. There was nothing insulting about Clementina's tone, yet the effect was offensive in the extreme. Daisy had only been trying to help things along by showing a friendly interest, and now she was left feeling inquisitive, and very small. Her mouse-face went bright pink, and she looked from Clementina to Bridget, in bewilderment.

'Very interesting,' said Bridget heavily. 'Mind-boggling in its fascination,' she couldn't resist adding. 'Come on, Daisy. Let's go and put the kettle on.'

Daisy got up, feeling foolish, and followed her downstairs.

3
The Old Tower

To make matters worse, Mrs Graham, when she came bouncing happily back from her trip to Glasgow, found Clementina delightful.

'You're not at all what I expected,' she announced with cheerful tactlessness, as she rushed around the kitchen, swathed in a large PVC apron, opening tins and sloshing their contents into dishes and pans. 'I thought you'd be a poor little waif in need of fattening up.' She paused in mid-flight, measured Clementina critically with her eye, and added, 'Well, maybe you do need fattening up, come to think of it. How much d'you weigh?'

'Six stone three,' said Clementina, who had brightened up as soon as Mrs Graham came into the house.

'Ridiculous,' pronounced Mrs Graham, who had a fat person's high regard for fat. 'It's unnatural. Can you peel potatoes?'

'Can I peel potatoes,' repeated Clementina feelingly.

'Right. Then do so. You'll find a peeler in the left-hand drawer, beside the sink – gold-plated, no doubt, in this place. Biddy, lay the table. I'm going to have my bath.'

She departed, shedding her apron, and silence fell over the kitchen. Neither Daisy nor Bridget was prepared to risk another snubbing; Bridget was in a bad temper, and showed it by dropping mats and cutlery on to the table from a great height. Daisy read a magazine, and Clementina peeled with absorption.

Presently Mrs Graham came down in a frilly frock, looking, Daisy could not help thinking disloyally, like a stout old Princess of Wales. The supper was put on to cook, and they all adjourned to the sitting-room, where Mrs Graham drank gin and tonic and chatted to Clementina, while Bridget and Daisy sat apart, eating peanuts in an aura of gloom. Clementina showed no reluctance to talk to Mrs Graham, who was, it seemed, an old friend of the house-parents at Torley Hall. It was because of this that Clementina had, at the last minute, been invited to join the holiday party at Benalmond.

'I must write to Annie Fowler and tell her you're undernourished,' said Mrs Graham teasingly. 'There are far too many skinny folk around, if you ask me. Really, between you and that shrimpy little Daisy, Biddy and I are going to feel positively mountainous, aren't we, Bid?'

Daisy could not help laughing out loud at the expression of outrage on Bridget's round face, but fortunately Bridget was too distracted to notice.

'I'm not fat,' she exploded. 'I'm exactly the correct weight for my height. I check it regularly.'

'Darling, I didn't realise you were so worried,' crooned her mother sympathetically.

Over supper, which was hearty enough to put flesh on a skeleton, Mrs Graham asked Clementina all about the school she went to, and about her music scholarship. Clementina answered with perfect candour questions which were much more probing than Daisy's had been earlier in the day.

'I have to practise my violin every morning,' she told Mrs Graham. 'You don't mind, do you?'

'Of course not, dear,' said Mrs Graham easily. 'We'll like to hear you play, won't we, girls? You can use my bedroom if you want to have a bit of privacy.'

She poured herself a second cup of coffee, put

in lots of sugar and cream, and turned to her daughter.

'Well, Biddy,' she went on. 'You're very quiet this evening. What have you and Daisy done today? Seen anything interesting?'

'In this weather?' enquired Bridget bitterly.

Daisy was never sure whether Mrs Graham genuinely didn't notice Bridget's moods, or chose to ignore them, because this was easier than getting involved in rows all the time. She suspected the latter, and, being a peaceful kind of person herself, now hurried to cover over Bridget's rudeness.

'We explored a bit in the morning, actually,' she said. 'There's a super swimming-pool, Mrs Graham, and an indoor games hall, and boats, a bit further along the loch side. And we had a look at that old tower place – the one we passed yesterday, coming in. Only from the outside, of course, because it's all locked up.'

Mrs Graham gave her a grateful look.

'I believe they're going to restore it,' she remarked. 'A good idea, really. It isn't beyond redemption yet, though it soon will be, if something isn't done quickly. There are a lot of places like it around, but any building that old is worth preserving, I think.'

'Well, I think it's sinister,' Daisy told her, recalling her feelings of the morning.

'Um,' said Mrs Graham, considering this. She was no more prone to atmospheric shivers than Bridget was. 'Well, perhaps it is. At any rate, it has been on fire at some point – possibly more than once. You can tell by the scorch marks on the stone. Rob Roy, maybe? It's his country around here.'

Mrs Graham was only speculating, without any great feeling of interest. Her knowledge of history was hazy, her concerns very much of the present. But she was anxious to ward off a quarrel with Bridget, which would have spoiled her pleasant day. Certainly she did not expect to be contradicted, but she was, with quiet authority.

'Oh, no. It wasn't Rob Roy,' said Clementina, 'although you're quite right about the burning, Mrs Graham. Monk's troops fired Benalmond in 1653, I've heard tell, and it was burned a second time after the 'Forty Five. It was the Redcoats who got the blame. Drummond was out with the Prince, you see.'

She seemed quite unaware that what she had said was in any way remarkable, even when three pairs of eyes, two pairs perplexed and one pair hostile, were turned towards her.

'Now, how on earth do you know all that, dearie?' asked Mrs Graham lightly. 'Have you been doing your homework?'

'Homework?' repeated Clementina, puzzled in her turn. Then she seemed to notice the interest her remarks had aroused, and as she looked at her companions her clear regard wavered. 'Well, yes. That is, I suppose I must have read it somewhere,' she concluded reluctantly.

Bridget had had a bad day, and this was the last straw. She could bear restraint no longer.

'Well, really,' she cried indignantly, banging the table with her fist. 'This very afternoon, you pretended —'

Her vehemence was cut short, decisively.

'That's enough, Bridget,' said Mrs Graham, getting up from the table, and beginning to draw the coffee cups and saucers towards her. 'Daisy and Clementina, go and get ready for bed, please. Bridget will help me with the washing-up tonight – your turn tomorrow. Run along, now.'

Nobody demurred.

Clementina went into the bathroom first. When Daisy had had her turn, and Bridget came stumping up to bed, she was lying with her face to the wall, pretending to be asleep. Daisy climbed into bed, and watched through half-shut eyes Bridget throwing off her clothes, shrugging on her night-dress, and flouncing under her quilt. In the darkness, Daisy lay curled into a miserable ball, wishing – and not for the last time – that she had refused the Grahams' invitation, and gone to the Manse at Crail for a month with her father and mother, and Simon and David and Rachel and Sarah and Ben.

Outside the wind blew, and the rain poured relentlessly down.

Bridget did not tell Daisy what had passed between her and her mother while they did the washing-up, but obviously she had been told to cool the situation, because next morning she had reverted to being reasonably polite to Clementina. This did not mean going out of her way to be friendly, but at least, Daisy noticed thankfully, she did not seem – for the time being, at least – to be spoiling actively for a fight. It was arranged – by Mrs Graham – that after breakfast Clementina would practise her music while Daisy wrote to her parents, and Bridget wrote some overdue birthday thank-you notes. Then, at eleven o'clock, they would meet, so that Clementina could be shown round the park by the other two. Clementina was acquiescent; she said she would be pleased to do whatever the other two wanted. But it was fairly obvious that the company of Bridget and Daisy was not what she longed for most in the world. Mrs Graham said she had work to do, and departed into the sitting-room, weighed down by several massive folders and a large mug of coffee.

'Lunch at one,' she told them, as she closed the door. 'Don't be early.'

Clementina collected her instrument and a sheaf of music from the communal bedroom, and went into Mrs Graham's room. As they laid out their writing pads and envelopes, and made themselves comfortable on top of their beds, Bridget and Daisy could hear through the wall the untuneful tuning-up of the violin.

'Preparing for a virtuoso performance of "O Can You Wash a Sailor's Shirt?" I suppose,' remarked Bridget sourly.

But nothing was further from the truth. Daisy, whose father loved music, and took her and Simon to concerts as often as he could afford it, quickly realised that Clementina was a really marvellous musician. Only a perfectionist, she knew, would have bothered to go over the part again and again, as Clementina did that morning. Anyone else would have been delighted with it the first time. But Daisy did not confide her thoughts to Bridget, who was shifting and tutting impatiently on her bed, writing and scoring out, crumpling sheets of paper and tossing them on the floor. She did, however, take the opportunity afterwards, while Bridget was in the loo, to say shyly to Clementina, 'You do play beautifully. I loved listening to you. That was a bit of Brahms' Violin Concerto, wasn't it?'

Clementina, who was putting her music away in a drawer, gave Daisy a surprised smile.

'Do you know it well?' she asked. 'Do you play at all yourself?'

Daisy hastened to assure her that she had neither knowledge nor talent.

'I have piano lessons, but I'm not much good,' she said. 'Dad takes me to concerts at the Music Hall sometimes – the Scottish National Orchestra, you know – that sort of thing.'

'Well, that's nice,' said Clementina. 'Most kids don't like anything but Pop.'

Bridget came back just then, so Daisy didn't say any more, but she noticed that when Clementina mentioned kids, she did not seem to include herself among them.

Perhaps it was different when you were nearly sixteen, thought Daisy, who was still three months short of her fourteenth birthday.

Downstairs in the kitchen, it seemed that Bridget – perhaps remembering that her mother was in the next room – was doing her best to appear civil. This did not prevent her dislike of Clementina from being obvious to Daisy, who only hoped that it wasn't obvious to Clementina too. Bridget poured three glasses of orange juice, and pressed ginger-snaps on Daisy and Clementina impartially. Then she asked Clementina if there were anything she'd especially like to do that morning. But of course, the answer was, 'No.'

'Then I suggest we just have a walk around,' said Bridget. 'And in the afternoon, we might go for a swim. How would that do?'

Clementina said it would do very well, if Daisy were agreeable, so they fetched their anoraks, and set off.

The rain had stopped at last, and in the damp summer heat mist was rising above the spiky forest roof, like floating smoke. The scented branches dripped steadily, but out of their shadow the ground was drying patchily, despite the absence of the sun. From banks of grass and wild flower rose the hum of busy insects, and as they walked along the girls had to avoid treading on worms and glistening black snails which were stranded in the wet runnels on either side of the paths.

Daisy and Bridget found themselves taking again the route they had followed yesterday, pointing out to Clementina the restaurant, the swimming-pool and the tennis-courts. Today there were other people around, mostly young, dressed in holiday clothes and carrying swimming gear, and cans of Coke. Some children passed them, kicking a football, then some boys on bicycles swooped around and said, 'Hello.' This had a cheering effect on Daisy and Bridget. Yesterday, Daisy remarked to Clementina, Benalmond had seemed like a deserted planet.

Eventually, they found themselves once again on the gravel in front of Benalmond Tower, but, this time, a surprise awaited them. The front door, which had looked as if it were bolted and sealed for evermore, now stood open. Beside it lay a heap of sawn planks, and a dirty metal skip, containing rubble and spikes of shattered wood. From the dark, dusty interior came the muffled sounds of sawing, hammering, and men's voices.

'They must have started work on the flats,' Bridget said. 'I wonder if we dare go in?'

'Do we want to?' asked Clementina, making the other two glance at her sharply.

But the remote, finely drawn face was giving nothing away; whatever strong feeling the Tower had aroused in Clementina the last time she saw it, she had it well under control now.

Daisy did not want to go in either, because of owls and bats and other fancies, but Bridget was very inquisitive, as well as unimaginative. So, when a workman, with a film of white dust over his hair and dungarees, came out to throw some wood into the skip, she approached him boldly.

'Is it all right if we take a look inside?' she asked.

His moustache and his eyelashes were white with dust too; that was all Daisy ever remembered about him. He looked at Bridget in some surprise, and replied, 'I dinna ken. It's no ma hoose. But it's no' nice inside. Ye'd dae better tae wait till we're feenished wi' it.'

He tossed his load of wood easily on to the skip with strong, sunburned arms.

But Bridget, being Bridget, was not to be put off.

'By that time it will belong to other people,' she persisted, 'and we won't be able to get in at all. Please?'

Daisy heard Clementina mutter impatiently, 'Oh, come on, for pity's sake. What does it matter?' But Bridget was giving her attention to the man.

He seemed to consider for a moment, but then he shook his head. 'Na. It's owre dangerous,' he said. 'There's nae licht in there, and if ye wis tae hae an accident, I wunna be held responsible. But if ye just wanted tae step in and hae a wee keek at the hallway – when ma back's turned, mind – there'd likely be nae harm.' He was moving away when another thought struck him, apparently, and he said over his shoulder, 'Wad ye no' be better goin' roond the back o' the place? That's whaur they keep the ponies.'

And before Bridget could say more, he was gone. They could hear him whistling, and his boots clattering off across the stone floor.

'Let's go and see the ponies,' suggested Daisy quickly.

'Good idea,' agreed Clementina, but Bridget was not to be diverted so easily.

'Later,' she said. 'All in good time. I want to see this place first. Then you'll get your ponies. Now, come on.'

Determinedly she led the way up the worn sandstone steps to the open door. Following unenthusiastically, Daisy and Clementina passed out of the warm, damp, grey outdoors into a cold, damp, grey cavern. Goose-pimples rose on their skin.

'What a very nasty place,' Daisy said, wrinkling up her small nose. 'Isn't it horrid, Clementina?'

Clementina nodded, but said nothing. She was standing with her shoulders hunched and her hands thrust down into the pockets of her green anorak, glancing about her with guarded eyes.

Even though there was no sunshine outside, it took some time for their sight to become adjusted to the even dimmer light within. Then they saw that they were standing in a large, unfurnished hall, with a vaulted roof supported by pillars of grey stone. The floor was flagged, and to left and right small archways opened into dark, low-ceilinged passages. Apart from the open doorway, the only sources of light were two narrow, slit-like windows, their glass unpleasantly furred with cobwebs and grime. The room was filthy, smelling of age, and stuffy, as places are which have been shut up for too long. The only interesting feature of the hall was a fireplace, which yawned like a great black mouth at the far end. Its sooty hearthstone, littered with small rubble and ancient bird droppings, was surrounded by an ornately carved stone chimney-piece, which claimed the girls' attention. In the centre a coat of arms was displayed, supported by unicorns like the ones on the gateposts at the entrance to the park. Peering closely, they saw that above this, on a small raised plaque, there was a date, 1750, and two intertwined initials, 'RD'.

'Drummond. Your friend, I suppose, who was "out with the Prince",' Bridget could not resist remarking to Clementina – much to Daisy's dismay. 'Are you able to tell us what his Christian name was too, or do you have to dash back for a quick peek into your crystal ball?'

Just for an instant, Daisy felt, quite inexplicably, that Clementina did know, and was going to retaliate by telling them. But then, 'Rumpelstiltskin,' she said, in a bored voice. 'Why don't you lay off, Bridget?'

'Let's go and see the ponies now,' put in Daisy, unnaturally loudly, before Bridget could make an angry reply.

'Right,' agreed Clementina calmly. 'They're at the back of the Tower, the man said. Come on.'

There was a little path on the right of the Tower, hacked out of a tangle of birch and rowan saplings. They followed it in single file, Clementina, Daisy, and an outraged Bridget in the rear. Presently they came to a rough finger-post which said, BENALMOND PONY-TREKKING CENTRE, then, beyond the wall of the Tower, to a stable-yard, and beyond that to a green enclosure with a wire fence round it. A number of ponies were quietly cropping the grass.

4

A Boy and a Horse

Benalmond Pony-Trekking Centre was like most other things at Benalmond, raw, makeshift and promising more for the future than could actually be delivered now. Against the rear wall of the Tower a row of loose boxes, like rough log cabins, had been erected to shelter the ponies; these were separated from the paddock by a wide, cemented yard, down one side of which stretched a kind of ranch house, with all its windows wide open to the air.

There were people around, though not many. Two boys and two girls, in jeans and wellingtons and waterproof waistcoats, were quietly busy mucking out the loose boxes, carrying large bundles of clean straw, and wheeling away barrows from which rose the unmistakable stable reek. Clementina, Daisy and Bridget leaned on the fence, watching the ponies. Two of them, shaggy little Shetlands with short legs and friendly eyes, came to greet them, nosing warmly in their hands for sugar. Daisy made up her mind that tomorrow they would not be disappointed. She would come again, with a supply of sugar lumps.

The sun had now decided to come out properly, and the surrounding forest was steaming up towards a pale blue sky.

'It's going to be a lovely day after all,' remarked Daisy, who was horribly oppressed by the angry silence.

But no one answered her, and they went on leaning on the fence.

However, all silences are broken, sooner or later, and this one was when one of the stable boys, apparently noticing them for the first time, straightened his back, thrust his fork into the smelly contents of his barrow, and came wading through the wet grass to speak to them.

'No riding today. Sorry,' he said. 'The Centre is always closed on Mondays to give the ponies a rest. Come back tomorrow, if you want to go out.'

He was a tall, fair-haired boy of about eighteen, in a red tartan shirt with the sleeves rolled up. He had a pleasant, grey-eyed face, tanned by sun and wind, and a long, strong body inside his scruffy clothes.

'We only came to look, actually,' Daisy said, believing herself to be the only one on speaking terms with anybody, 'although we would like to ride some time, while we're here.'

The boy was opening his mouth to reply when Bridget, who never liked to let Daisy take the initiative, cut in with, 'Can you tell us something about it? I mean, how much does it cost, and what gear do we have to have?'

The boy climbed on to the fence, and sat balancing himself with one leg over the top of a wooden post.

'It's a pound an hour, if you want to do it that way,' he said. 'If you want a whole day's trek, it costs a fiver, which is better value, and more fun. The best thing is to come on one of our three-day camps – we run one every week. Sometimes we go up Loch Lomond side, but more often we go up through the forest to Glenfinglas, and make our way home around Loch Katrine and through the hills. We don't cover great distances – it's better to take your time, and have stops, and enjoy looking at things as you go along. We usually stop and make camp fairly early, so that we can see to the ponies, and have a good supper and a bit of a singsong round the fire before we turn in.'

He did not speak like a person trying to sell something, but rather like someone recalling thoroughly good times. His enthusiasm was infectious. Still —

'How much?' demanded practical Bridget.

'Fifteen quid. And you have to bring a share of the food.'

Daisy calculated quickly and thankfully that her holiday pocket-money would easily stretch that far. She could think of nothing more agreeable than getting away from the chalet by the loch, and meeting other young people. Even if she could not escape from Bridget and Clementina altogether, she thought – with a twinge of conscience at her own disloyalty – at least their company would be less oppressive in the open air, with other people around.

'What clothes do we need?' she asked anxiously, thinking of the Majorca-type finery they had foolishly brought for this country holiday, and how unsuitable it was likely to be for anything they wanted to do.

The boy ran his eye over them, assessing the warmth of their clothing, and how waterproof it was likely to be.

'What you've got on will be fine,' he said, 'provided you have a warm jersey with you in your pack. No wellies allowed, but you can hire boots, and you get a hard hat on loan as part of the package.'

But his voice had changed, as if he were no longer interested in answering their questions – and simultaneously, Bridget and Daisy realised why. His scrutiny had frozen when it reached Clementina, and now he was looking at her, and she was looking at him, as if they wanted to go on looking for ever. Bridget and Daisy felt as if they were no longer there, an experience both annoying and embarrassing.

'When does the next camp start?' asked Bridget loudly, to break their spell.

The boy came back reluctantly, from a far distance.

'Wednesday. Always Wednesday,' he replied. And to Clementina, anxiously, 'You'll come, won't you?'

'Of course, Angus,' she said.

It was another of those awkward moments when no one knew quite what to say, although Daisy knew that Bridget would have plenty to say later, in private. Clementina stood with her hands in her pockets, looking at the boy, and only the tiniest flicker of anxiety in her eyes betrayed the fact that she had frightened herself.

'What makes you think my name is Angus?' asked the boy, half jokingly.

'Is it?'

'Yes.'

'You look like an Angus,' Clementina told him lightly.

'You mean it was just a brilliant guess?'

'I suppose so. What else could it have been?'

Angus jumped down from the fence, on the paddock side, and grinned at her.

'Guess my surname,' he challenged her, laughing.

If she knew, Clementina was now on her guard.

'Pumblechook,' she said, warding off danger, as she had in the Tower.

'Not so. Try again.'

'MacWheeble, then.'

'Have a heart. Guess seriously.'

'Oh, I don't know. Marshall.'

'Wrong. It's Wishart. What's yours?'

'Clementina Rattray.'

'That's a mouthful. Doesn't anybody call you Tina?'

'Certainly not.'

'Then I will.'

He did not ask Daisy and Bridget their names, which made them feel more than ever that they were not there.

They arrived back at the chalet for lunch, Bridget furious, and even mild little Daisy a trifle piqued.

Mrs Graham, who was certainly having a more enjoyable holiday than anyone else, so far, had moved on to the verandah overlooking the loch when the sun came out, and was sitting with her feet up on a wicker *chaise longue*, drinking her pre-lunch gin and tonic, and reading the *Guardian*. She put the paper down when the three girls came up the steps, and beamed cheerfully at them.

'Had a lovely morning?' she asked, then, fortunately not waiting for a reply, went on, 'There's white wine in the fridge, if you'd like a glass. Clementina, be a love and bring it out. I'll have another gin.'

Daisy, who was never allowed anything even mildly alcoholic at home, sat down on the wooden steps, feeling sophisticated, and held up her face to the sun. Bridget said she was going to change, and departed indoors.

'Have there been any fights this morning?' Mrs Graham whispered to Daisy.

'Two,' Daisy told her.

'They don't like each other,' said Mrs Graham, as if this were more amusing than otherwise.

'No,' agreed Daisy.

Mrs Graham was silent for a moment, then she sighed, and said, 'Biddy is so quick-tempered. Exactly like her father, of course.'

With this Daisy could neither agree nor disagree. She had never met Mr Graham, from whom Mrs Graham was divorced, and who was understood to be living in California. At least, it was from there that extravagant International Money Orders arrived for Bridget, at Christmas, and on her birthday. At other times she never mentioned her father. Daisy was saved from the necessity of a reply to Mrs Graham by the appearance of

Clementina, carrying a tray with their drinks. Daisy took her glass and sipped the cold, sour liquid, assuring herself that she was enjoying it.

Not surprisingly, perhaps, Clementina was now more enthusiastic about the pony-trekking idea than were the other two, but, when questioned by Mrs Graham, they both said that they would like to go. Daisy still wanted to get away from the present situation if she could, and Bridget was already thinking secretly how nice it would be if she could lure Angus Wishart away from Clementina. Mrs Graham, however, would not agree to their going to the three-day camp this week; with unusual concern she insisted that they must accustom themselves gradually to life in the saddle.

'After all, you've had no riding experience, any of you,' she pointed out. 'Think how sore your poor behinds would be, with all that bumping up and down. No – you must begin with an hour at a time, and work up gradually from there. Perhaps every second day to begin with, and a day's trek next week – then you'll be ready to enjoy the camp properly the week after that.'

'But I can't afford to do it that way,' objected Daisy. 'The camp alone costs fifteen pounds, and I've only got twenty-eight pounds fifty. I've got to buy presents for all my brothers and sisters out of that.'

'The same goes for me,' said Clementina regretfully. 'I've got thirty pounds with me, and although I could get more if I wrote to Mrs Fowler, I'd really rather not. I'm saving up my allowance to start me off in London.'

'No problems at all,' Mrs Graham assured them. 'You pay for your hour-long rides, and I'll stand you a day's trek, and the camp as a treat, nearer the end of the holiday. It'll be well worth it to get rid of you all for four days,' she added with her usual candour, and, because they had no doubt at all that she was speaking the truth, the girls accepted her offer.

The next day was beautiful, all sunshine and blue sky, and the loch lightly ruffled by a slight, summery breeze. Again Clementina practised her music in Mrs Graham's untidy, scented bedroom, but, after the other two had waited patiently for her downstairs, offended them by refusing to go swimming with them. She would rather go for a walk by herself, she said, and, having put on her boots because of the wetness of the forest floor, off she went. Bridget was bitterly convinced that her walk would take her no further than the Pony-Trekking Centre, but she could not prove this without following her, which would be undignified. So she went grumbling to the swimming-pool with Daisy. They swam, had a coffee in the restaurant, and came home.

In the afternoon, they all three went up to the Pony-Trekking Centre for their first ride. A number of other young people, boys and girls aged between nine and twenty, were already queuing outside a small office at one end of the ranch house; the girls joined the queue, which moved slowly. They paid their pounds, and were directed towards another small room, smelling of new wood and leather. There, after a bit of trying on and discarding, with grimaces of discomfort, they were equipped with hard riding hats and leather boots, and directed to the paddock. Angus and another young man were waiting for them with a group of docile, slightly bored looking ponies, already saddled from their last outing. Each rider was allocated a pony of roughly the right height, and told its name; Bridget's grey pony was called Coxy, Daisy's brown and white one was called Tam. They settled themselves somewhat gingerly into the saddle, holding the reins in unaccustomed hands. They need not have worried, however. These ponies were schooled to obedience, and bore their riders patiently, if without enthusiasm. Daisy was wiggling her feet in the stirrups, and patting Tam's neck in the hope of making friends with him, when she heard Bridget say, 'Oh, God,' between her teeth, and turned to see what was the matter now.

Clementina, who had been last in the queue, was holding everyone up by having an argument with Angus. She was refusing to mount the brown pony he was holding for her, and they could hear her saying vehemently, 'No, Angus. No. I want that one,' while pointing to a larger, darker animal which was cropping the grass some distance away.

Angus was refusing, with equal determination.

'Sorry, Tina,' he said. 'That's Billy. He's a bad-tempered devil, and we never allow clients to ride him. It would be asking for trouble.'

'Why is he saddled, then?'

'Because I'm going to ride him myself,' Angus explained. 'He needs a firm hand, that one, and he and I know each other. You take Tinker, there's a good girl.'

'But Angus, I know I could —'

'*No*, Tina. Sorry and all that, but you'd have an accident, and I'd get the blame.'

'People are looking,' growled Bridget, as indeed they were – and it is, as everyone knows, a shocking breach of good manners in Scotland to cause people to look.

Clementina herself must have realised this, because suddenly she capitulated.

'All right,' she said, allowing Angus to help her to mount Tinker, and show her how to hold the reins.

But her face was flushed and troubled as the other boy – 'Call me Mick,' he told them cheerfully – began to lead the string of ponies out of the paddock and under the forest eaves. Without urging, Tam and Coxy and Tinker followed the line, and were a little way into the wood before Angus and Billy caught up with them.

It was a perfect summer afternoon, and nothing – had one perhaps been a little happier inside oneself – could have been more delightful than an hour's ride through the forest, at one moment dark and damp and mysteriously resinous, soft and silent as a deep-piled carpet under the ponies' hoofs, the next in full sunlight as the conifers fell suddenly away, and they emerged on to a sunken track between walls of bramble and bracken. There the only trees were small, scrubby birches, and wind-twisted rowans, their pale orange berries clustering among tremulous leaves. Sometimes they crossed a stream, clear and clean as it bubbled busily over stones between banks of heather. Daisy tried to enjoy it, and reminded herself crossly how bored she had been on the beach at Crail last year, and the year before that, and the year before that. But Bridget's large and huffy back, bumping along on Coxy just in front of her, and Clementina's voice, chatting quietly to Angus just behind, could not be ignored; Daisy found herself wondering how it would be if she simply went back to the chalet, packed her suitcase, and said she was leaving . . . only she knew she wouldn't, of course. The upset would be so awful, it was easier to stick it out to the end. At least, that was how it seemed, at the time.

It was apparent, from the talking and laughing at the rear of the column, that Angus and Clementina had not fallen out over the affair of the pony, Billy. Angus rode him well, with firm hands on the reins, but, Daisy noticed on the two occasions when Angus moved down the side of the column to speak to Mick, Billy did not behave like any of the other ponies. His head tossed and his eye was unsteady, and he kicked out nervously with his back legs if there was an unexpected sound, or movement in the grass. Daisy thought that Clementina had been wise to give in; it was plain that Billy was not a mount for an inexperienced rider. However, when, at the end of the hour, they arrived back at base, a very odd thing happened.

All the riders had dismounted, and already the ponies were being led away by two of the other grooms to where a new queue was forming. But suddenly Billy, who had been turned loose by Angus at a safe distance from the group, turned round, and began to trot purposefully back in their direction. Before either Angus or Mick could stop her, Clementina had stepped confidently towards him, had taken him by the bridle, and was patting his nose, talking to him in a caressing, familiar manner. And even as Mick shouted angrily, 'Get back, you stupid girl, he'll bite you,' Billy's head stopped twitching, his eye calmed, and he put down his hairy black mouth to nuzzle Clementina's shoulder, and the palm of her hand.

Distanced by their shared astonishment, Angus and Mick and Bridget and Daisy watched, while the other riders drifted away across the grass. Mick emitted a low, puzzled whistle, but it was Angus who moved over to Clementina, and gently took the bridle from her hand.

'All right,' he said. 'You win. And you say you have no experience with horses.'

'I haven't,' said Clementina. 'Oh, and by the way, his name isn't Billy. It's Gib. You should have known that.'

With which she went off in the direction of the ranch house, to return her borrowed hat and boots.

5
Aggro

'That girl,' said Bridget emphatically, 'is either a liar or a witch.'

It was the flat hour between supper and bedtime, when there was not time to do anything much, but it was too early to start thinking about baths, and hair washing, and getting ready for the night. Mrs Graham was having a long gossip on the telephone with her neighbour in Aberdeen, who was feeding the cats, and Clementina was sitting on the verandah with a clip-board on her lap, writing a letter to the Fowlers. At least, that was what she said she was doing. Most of the time she seemed to be playing idly with her pen, and staring absently at the setting sun. Bridget and Daisy, having strolled to the landing-stage and back, were now down by the loch in front of the chalet, skimming flat stones across the water. Bridget was much better at it than Daisy was.

Daisy watched her stone bounce once, half-heartedly, and sink below the waves. She looked at Bridget out of the corner of her eye, and asked, 'Do you believe in witches?'

'No. You know what I believe,' said Bridget defensively.

'That's an awful thing to say about anybody,' said Daisy in a low voice. She wandered up the shore, her little brown face creased with anxiety, and sat down on a bank of crumbly sand, under some birch trees. Bridget skimmed another couple of stones, then came to join her.

'It's all very well looking shocked, my dear,' she said, flopping down at Daisy's feet. 'But can you think of another explanation? I mean – how could she possibly know all these things about Benalmond Tower if she hasn't read them, or – far more likely if you ask me – been here before? And as for that pony, Billy – well, it was obvious, wasn't it? He knew her. Now, if she's honest, why the hell doesn't she just come clean? That's what I'd like to know.'

'She hadn't met Angus before,' Daisy pointed out. 'But she knew his name. How do you explain that?'

'I suppose she's allowed one correct guess,' conceded Bridget grudgingly.

Daisy picked up a handful of silver sand, and let it trickle slowly through her fingers.

'I don't think she's been here before,' she said eventually. 'It's too unlikely, Bid. This is the first year this place has been open, and there's no reason I can see why someone in her situation should have come here before it became a holiday centre. Besides —'

'Besides what?'

'Well – I've had the feeling, every time she's come out with one of these odd remarks, that she has frightened herself, somehow.'

'So you think it's witchcraft?' demanded Bridget, challengingly.

'No, of course not,' said Daisy, horrified, as she got up hastily, and went off to wash her hair.

She did not, then or at any other time, think it was witchcraft; that was a word she associated on the one hand with steeple hats and Hallowe'en parties, and on the other, vaguely, with unspeakable things practised long ago. But always, afterwards, she remembered that night as the first time she had admitted, unwillingly, to herself that something might be happening which could not be explained by saying that a girl you scarcely knew was telling lies.

Against all Daisy's expectations, however, the atmosphere during the next day or two definitely improved. The good weather continued, and the girls were out of doors from early morning until the sun went down, golden and glorious, reddening the mountain peaks and turning the little loch to a basin of fragmented fire. Daisy and Clementina turned a rich, sun-flushed brown, and even Bridget's fair skin acquired a little of the tan she longed for. Clementina, fortunately for harmony, made no more inexplicable remarks, and because they were busy, and not cooped up together, the three uneasy companions managed to put up with one another. One day they went sailing, another they rode, not through the forest this time, but round the loch to a little village called Vingen, where they stopped for ice cream. Angus and Billy, they heard, were away at Rowardennan on a three-day camp, and they were escorted by Mick and a girl groom called Wendy. In between times they swam, and sunbathed, and played golf; they were all so hilariously bad at golf that their badness almost made a bond between them. When Clementina bought Bridget a can of Coke after swimming, and Bridget lent Clementina her current copy of *Honey* magazine, Daisy even wondered if all might yet be well. But that, of course, was asking too much.

The weather broke on Friday evening with a most spectacular thunderstorm. In the morning, they woke to the old, familiar sound of muffled drumming on the shingled roof, and a persistent 'Plip, plip, plop,' as water fell from the eaves on to the wooden verandah below. When Daisy got up and drew aside the curtains, she saw the loch, black and uninviting under a low roof of cloud, the mountains were completely blotted out.

'This is where we came in,' she remarked to the other two, as she put on her dressing-gown and shuffled about, feeling for her slippers with her bare toes.

'It isn't worth getting up at all,' Bridget growled, pulling the duvet over her head. 'I've had an awful night with my bites,' she added pathetically. 'I think I'll have a lie in.'

Bridget had been bitten, the previous day, by a horde of midges and clegs; against everyone's advice she had allowed herself the passing pleasure of a good scratch, and had been paying for it ever since.

'Well, I must get up,' said Clementina, pushing her long brown feet over the edge of the bed. 'I'll have to do some extra practice today. I've been neglecting work for the good life. I hope Harriet isn't having a lie in too, Bridget.'

Mrs Graham had invited both Clementina and Daisy to call her Harriet. Clementina had proceeded to do so; Daisy had been so embarrassed that she had since avoided addressing her by any name at all.

Bridget watched balefully through a chink in the bedclothes, as Clementina combed her hair and slipped on her dressing-gown. One of the things that irked Bridget about Clementina was the way she looked when she got up in the morning, fresh and tidy and clear-eyed, instead of sleepy and rumpled, like Bridget.

'Someone might bring me up a cup of coffee and some toast,' she said peevishly.

'Sure,' agreed Clementina, but, unfortunately, forgot to do so.

Mrs Graham was not having a lie in. When Daisy and Clementina arrived downstairs for breakfast, she was getting ready to set off for Glasgow, where she had another lunch appointment.

'Have a lovely day,' she said absent-mindedly, as she

buttoned up her waterproof and searched in all her pockets for the car-keys. 'Don't drown.' She found the keys, wiggled her fingers at them, and departed.

'What a woman,' said Clementina admiringly.

Left to themselves, they had a day of what Mrs Graham called 'aggro'. This was a word which seemed to cover a great deal of grousing and bitching and failing to live in peace with other people.

As soon as she had swallowed her orange juice and toast, Clementina went upstairs to Mrs Graham's room. She had finished her work on Brahms' Violin Concerto, and had begun practising a very modern piece by a Bulgarian composer with an unpronounceable name. To both Bridget and Daisy, it was quite unrecognisable as music at all. Bridget had said so; Daisy, who was anxious to retain her reputation with Clementina as a person of musical taste, had said she supposed it might grow on you, to which Clementina had replied that she didn't think it would ever grow on her. Now, they had to put up with two hours of cacophony. It was bad enough for Daisy, curled up in the sitting-room with *The Heart of Midlothian* – all five hundred and forty-eight pages of which she had to read for school next term – on her knee; for Bridget, lying through the wall, tossing and itching and trying to get to sleep, the experience was a maddening one. When, at half-past ten, the girl who came to help with the housework arrived, and began to Hoover, she could bear it no longer, and came stumping down to the kitchen to cook herself bacon and eggs. Daisy heard much muttering about ghastly noise and selfish beasts, and knew that the truce was over.

The rest of the day was made miserable by Bridget's moans about her bites, and the weather, and the awfulness of absolutely everything. After lunch, Clementina disappeared, and at four o'clock, unable to bear Bridget's complaining any longer, Daisy too put on her waterproof, and went for a long walk in the rain. When she came back, she brought the news that there was to be a disco that evening at the games hall; she was not a great lover of discos, but sheer desperation made her suggest to Bridget that they should go. Bridget, who did enjoy discos, agreed at once.

'It's a pity we can't lose Miss Fiddle, though,' she said regretfully. 'We'll have to ask her – Mother will kick up a fuss if we don't.'

But Clementina's reaction to a grudging invitation, when she came back wet and shining from her outing, was offhand.

'Oh, yes. I was going to tell you about it, actually. I am going – Angus asked me.'

She did not say where, or when, he had asked her, but Bridget's long-held suspicion that Clementina 'sneaked off' to the Trekking Centre now seemed confirmed.

'See? What did I tell you?' she said disagreeably to Daisy, after Clementina had gone upstairs. 'Going for a walk, my eye. You'll notice she only has time for us when Mr Wishart is away at a three-day camp. Ah well, we'll see.'

She did not say what they would see, and Daisy did not ask her. She went up to change, thinking that this was the most tiresome day she had ever spent in her life. And it was not over yet.

Mrs Graham, when she came home at half-past five, was delighted to hear that they were all going out. She said that she wanted to watch a programme on television about child deprivation in India, then she would have an early night.

'I'm worn out trying to be clever in German,' she said. 'Of course, they all speak perfect English, but it's letting the side down, don't you think, not to try to speak to people in their own language? Pour me a gin, Biddy, then I'll think about scrambling some eggs.'

She did not say anything about being in by eleven, or keeping together on the way home; it still came as a shock to Daisy to realise that Mrs Graham honestly didn't care where they went, or what they did, as long as they left her in peace.

Bridget spent so long in the bathroom that Daisy was getting really impatient, and she could see that Clementina was too, from the way she kept glancing at her watch, and drumming with her fingers on the edge of the kitchen table. But when Bridget did come down, Daisy had to admit that she looked marvellous, in a fashionable blue silky frock, with her face nicely made up, and her thick fair hair swept up and knotted on top of her head. Bridget was a pretty girl, with a clear, pink and white skin and wide blue eyes; it was a pity that so often her face was spoiled by a sulky expression. But now, when Daisy said, 'Gosh, you do look super, Bid,' she smiled, because that was what she wanted to hear.

Clementina said, 'Come on, then. It's getting awfully late,' and they walked up through the damp wood, hearing the disco music beating ever more urgently in the still air, as they neared the games hall.

The dance was well under way when they went in; the lights flashed in the darkness and the atmosphere which Daisy loathed swathed itself around them, smelling of bodies and smoke and cheap scent. Almost at once, Angus Wishart materialised out of the shadows. He said, 'Hello, there,' to Daisy and Bridget, and to Clementina, 'I thought you were lost. Let's go to the cafeteria and have something to drink before we dance – it's as hot as hell in here.'

He said it pointedly to Clementina; it was not a general invitation, and Daisy was already peering into the gloom, trying to spot some of the boys and girls they had met sailing, or at the swimming-pool, when to her dismay she saw that Bridget had got on the other side of Angus, and was accompanying him and Clementina across the hall to the cafeteria door. By the time Daisy had decided that she had better go too, if only to get Bridget away, they were separated from her by a mass of jerking bodies; when she caught up with them, Clementina and Bridget were seated at a table, and Angus was at the counter, buying them lemonade. Bridget waved brightly to Daisy, calling, 'We're over here! Come and join us!' and Daisy, feeling ill with embarrassment, crept across to the table.

'John Orr and the Morrisons are in the hall,' she said hopefully to Bridget, who had seemed rather keen on Robert Morrison when they had met at the pool. 'Why don't we join them?'

'Oh, later, maybe,' Bridget said airily. 'The night is young.'

Daisy gritted her teeth, and did not know whether to feel better or worse when she saw Clementina smiling at her; it was a mocking smile, more likely than not.

The next hour was terrible. Angus, looking resigned, danced with Bridget, then with Clementina, then with Daisy. After that, Daisy felt she could bear it no longer, and when Bridget had ignored her second broad hint, took herself off to join Robert and Anne Morrison and their friends, who were in a huddle on the other side of the hall. They all seemed pleased to see her, and, despite the noise and the heat, she could have enjoyed herself, had she not been seeing constantly, through gaps in the dancing throng, Bridget in her expensive blue dress, smiling at Angus, talking to Angus, dancing opposite Angus. Angus was being far more polite than Bridget deserved, but Daisy knew, and Bridget ought to have known, that all he really wanted was to be left alone with Clementina. She, as usual, was looking like a swan among hens in her plain white blouse and denim skirt, with her sunburnt feet thrust into the cheapest of canvas shoes.

Finally, they got rid of Bridget quite simply. They went separately to the loo, and didn't come back. Daisy saw Bridget moving fretfully up and down on the margin of the dance floor; eventually, realising that she was alone, she came across to Daisy's group, and set about attracting the attention of Robert Morrison. Unfortunately, he by that time had been attracted by someone else, so Bridget did not get very far with him, either. She danced once or twice with one of the other boys, then said abruptly to Daisy, 'I've had enough of this. I'm going home.'

So Daisy went with her. It was easier than risking a row by saying she would prefer to stay.

The clouds had rolled away, and they walked back through the wood with a white slice of moon weaving itself into the lattice of branches overhead. The music faded behind them, to be replaced by the kindlier sounds of the falling night, birds settling fussily on to their perches, a little wind breathing in the leaves.

'I just wish I could think of some way of getting her to go,' said Bridget, moodily kicking a pine cone along the path. 'She's ruining our holiday. But it's no use talking to Mother. She never listens to a word I say.'

Daisy knew that now was the time to defend Clementina, to point out that there was nothing you could tell Mrs Graham that would be true. Clementina was more reserved than one might wish, but she had not really done anything wrong; Bridget was jealous, for no good reason, and was spoiling things for herself. But, as usual, Daisy's courage failed her. Instead, she said hesitantly, 'Do you really like Angus Wishart very much, Bid?'

She watched Bridget bridle.

'Angus Wishart?' she repeated incredulously. 'Angus

Wishart? Of course not. Whatever gave you that idea? I only wanted —' Bridget stopped short. Perhaps she realised that she was about to give too much away. Then, 'Come on. I'll race you back to the chalet,' she said.

It was well after eleven when Clementina came back. They could hear her and Angus whispering and laughing on the verandah under the open window. Words floated up to them.

'Tomorrow, then. Promise.'

'No. I must practise.'

'Monday, then.'

'Yes, all right. But do be quiet now. You'll wake them up.'

A pause.

'Once more, then. Just once more.'

Another pause.

'No, that's enough. Ssh, Angus!'

They heard the door creaking as Clementina opened it stealthily, and Clementina's feet, gentle on the uncarpeted stair. Then a crunchy thud, as Angus jumped over the verandah railing on to the shingle, and cheerful whistling as he bounded away, not really caring whom he woke up. When Clementina softly turned the handle of the bedroom door, and slipped inside, both Bridget and Daisy were pretending to be asleep.

6
Charlie's Room

Clementina came downstairs on Monday morning in the clothes she wore to go riding. After breakfast, she told Mrs Graham that she had arranged to spend the day with a friend at the Trekking Centre, and would not be in to lunch. Mrs Graham laughed, and winked at her broadly, but all she said was, 'But what about music? Hath it no charms today?'

'I practised all day yesterday. I'm giving myself a holiday today,' said Clementina, and departed.

It was a parting of the ways, really. From then on, she did as she pleased, and the pretence that she was sharing a holiday with Bridget and Daisy was abandoned by everybody.

Bridget had managed to infect a bite on her ankle rather badly, by scratching it, and was demanding to see a doctor. Mrs Graham was not averse to this proposal, until she realised that she would have to provide the transport.

'What's that, Daisy? The doctor only consults at Aberfoyle? Oh, damn. Well then, couldn't you hop, Biddy? Oh, I see. It's two and a half miles, and you'd die by the wayside. What a bore. I suppose I'll have to get the car out, and take you.'

'What a lovely mummy,' said Bridget angrily.

Daisy was delighted to see them go, and hoped there would be a long queue. Revelling in the unaccustomed peace, she gathered up the breakfast dishes, washed them, and tidied up the kitchen. Unfortunately, she had scarcely finished when she heard the car arriving back, and Bridget entered, bandaged and limping solemnly.

'It was touch and go for crutches,' said Mrs Graham to Daisy, laughing merrily as she put on the kettle for more coffee.

Bridget spent the rest of the day lolling on the sofa in the sitting-room, with her foot on a cushion. Daisy felt obliged by good manners to stay with her, although privately she agreed with Mrs Graham that Bridget was making a great deal more fuss than was necessary. Daisy was bored to distraction by Bridget's railing against Clementina; it was as if Angus and Clementina had become friends with no other purpose than to annoy Bridget. It did not matter how often Daisy tried to turn the conversation to other matters, Bridget turned it back to Clementina, her dishonesty and her furtive love affair. For the life of her, Daisy couldn't see what was furtive about it; it seemed to her that everybody knew. But she knew better than to irritate Bridget still further by supporting the other side.

It was a long, long day, and supper-time before they all came together again, around the kitchen table. Mrs Graham had made goulash, and a strawberry meringue sponge. She was a very good cook, when she could be bothered. There was silence while they all ate heartily, but then, while they were loosening their belts and waiting for the coffee to percolate, Mrs Graham suddenly snapped her fingers and said, 'There now! I knew I had something interesting to tell you. Listen to this!'

They all sat up, and took notice.

'When I was in Glasgow on Saturday,' Mrs Graham began, 'I happened to be in a bookshop, and I picked up a book about Central Perthshire – a sort of illustrated guidebook, you know. It was reduced from nine pounds ninety-five to two pounds fifty, so I bought it – thought we might as well have some education on the cheap, so to speak. Well, fascinating isn't the word for it, my dears. You remember I was going to have an early night, to restore the bloom of youth and beauty? What a hope. I took it up to bed with me, and I was still reading it when Clementina came crashing home with her boy-friend. There's a long section on the history of the Drummonds of Benalmond – you were right, Clementina, that was their name – and a proper crowd of silly billies they were too, always backing the wrong side, and getting themselves into trouble.'

'The Stuarts weren't the wrong side, Harriet,' said Clementina coolly, drawing a sharp glance from Bridget, but by this time Mrs Graham was in full flight.

'You were also right about the Tower being set on fire after the Seventeen Forty Five Rebellion,' she continued, beaming at Clementina as at a pupil who had done well, 'but it wasn't an official act of revenge, or anything like that. A detachment of Redcoat soldiers, on their way back south from Culloden, decided to demand Lady Drummond's hospitality while her husband was away. There wasn't a lot she could do about it, poor soul. In the course of the evening, they got completely drunk, on the absent Drummond's wine and ale, of course, and the story goes that they managed to set fire to the stables when they went out to see to their horses. It was bitterly cold, and the streams were all frozen, so there was no water to put the fire out. Also, the stables were attached to the house, and the wind blew burning thatch on to the roof. By morning, the whole place was reduced to a shell.'

'How awful. Was anyone killed?' asked Daisy in a small voice. She was always frightened by stories of fires.

'One servant, two horses,' Mrs Graham told her. 'No Redcoats, which seems a trifle unfair. However,' she went on, smacking the edge of the table triumphantly with the palm of her hand, 'that's not really what I set out to tell you. There's something else, an odd coincidence, in present company. Lady Drummond was a Miss Rattray before she married. Miss Arabella Rattray of Generoch, heiress of great estates in the north. A definite cut above the Drummonds, if you ask me. So there you are, Clementina. Maybe you're connected to the rich and famous. What do you think?'

'A likely story,' Clementina replied.

Both Bridget and Daisy were watching her as she got up, and fetched the coffee-pot from the hotplate, but, if any of this tale were familiar to her, she was keeping her face well under control. Too well under control, perhaps. There was a tightness about her mouth, as she poured the coffee, and she suddenly looked tired, and older than she was. Daisy felt very sorry for her.

But then Clementina put down the coffee-pot, faced Mrs Graham, and said with great deliberation, 'My Rattrays were fishmongers in Dundee, Harriet. There's nothing very aristocratic about that. I have nothing to do with the Drummonds of Benalmond, and I don't want to have – they mean nothing to me at all. Is that quite clear?'

'Perfectly, dear,' said Mrs Graham, looking slightly offended. 'You don't have to convince me.'

It sounded to Daisy more as though she was trying to convince herself.

Partly out of curiosity, and partly out of politeness, Daisy borrowed the book from Mrs Graham and took it up to bed with her. She lay in her little pine bed with her back to the others, turning the pages nervously, almost as if she was afraid of reading something she didn't want to know. But there wasn't much that Mrs Graham had not already told them. Arabella, Lady Drummond, had rebuilt the Tower house in 1750, after her husband's flight to France in the wake of Bonnie Prince Charlie. Her son, her grandson and her great-grandson had all lived there. But then, in 1890, the Drummonds had removed to a more modern house near Balquhidder, and the life had gone out of Benalmond. There were some interesting photographs, including one of an 1800 engraving of the Tower house, surrounded by a formal garden, and another of the coat of arms which they had seen above the chimney-piece in the hall. Above were the twined initials, 'RD'.

'Clementina,' Daisy said.

'Mn?'

'Remember that plaque we saw in the Tower, with 'RD 1750' on it? The 'R' stands for Rattray. It wasn't Drummond's Christian name after all.'

'Mn,' said Clementina again, twitching up her duvet, and snapping off her light.

Daisy put out her light too, and lay for a while in the frail summer darkness, thinking of many things, and able to understand none of them. Bridget had fallen asleep straight away; you could always tell by the way she breathed whether she was really sleeping, or whether she was pretending. Perhaps she was very tired, after sleeping so badly recently, Daisy thought, with a twinge of self-reproach at the memory of her own annoyance with Bridget during the day. She thought that Clementina was asleep too, and indeed, afterwards, supposed she must have been, for one couldn't imagine Clementina saying what she did when she was even half awake. Yet the words were perfectly clear, not sleepy at all.

'It wasn't the Redcoats, Angus. They didn't go back to the stables. It was Charlie. I know it was Charlie.'

Then Clementina sighed, turned over, and said no more.

It was provoking that now, when everyone else, for one reason or another, would have been happy to forget about the Tower, Mrs Graham should develop an enthusiasm for history. For the next couple of days, she was for ever reading aloud passages from her book, and obviously considered it a great feather in her cap when she managed to gain permission for them all to explore inside the Tower. She had been up to the shop by the swimming-pool for tonic water, she told them when she came panting back, and on the way, passing the Tower, she had met such a nice man, who had passed the time of day, and who had turned out to be the contractor in charge of the renovations.

'You mean you waylaid him, don't you, Mother?' asked Bridget, who, recovered from her injury, was practising yoga positions on the verandah.

'Not at all,' said Mrs Graham, with dignity. 'He spoke first. I merely replied. Anyway,' she went on, choosing to ignore the wide grin on every face, 'I asked him if there were any reason why my daughter and her friends, who were passionately interested in history, shouldn't have a look inside. His name's Jerry Briggs, by the way. He said there was no reason at all, provided that I went with you, and we didn't touch any of the things lying about. He suggests we go this afternoon, when the workmen will be away at a Union meeting at Buchlyvie – where on earth's Buchlyvie? I've to pick up a key from the Estate Office, any time after two.'

'And he's taking you out for a drink this evening,' said Bridget.

'No, to lunch on Sunday,' said Mrs Graham, and was offended when everyone laughed.

Daisy and Bridget had intended to play golf that afternoon, and Clementina to ride with Angus, but none of them wanted to disappoint Mrs Graham, who obviously thought she had done them a really good turn. So, after lunch, they went with her to the Estate Office to collect the key, and, each with her own thoughts locked away behind an interested face, followed her into the Tower.

The room they had been in earlier, with its impressive stone fireplace, was now dirtier than ever, full of doors and pieces of ripped-out woodwork, with a film of white dust over all. The acrid smell of the dust filled the air, so that your nose felt unpleasantly dry, and every step aroused a little cloud which then settled back, all over your shoes and the bottoms of your trousers. They paused so that Mrs Graham could examine the coat of arms by the light of a large torch which she had brought, then they went out, in single file, by the archway on the right of the fireplace. The dust stopped a few feet down the vaulted passage; evidently the restoration work had been begun on the other side of the house.

Benalmond Tower was not like any old castle the girls had visited before. They had expected bare stone walls, and uncovered floors, and airy emptiness. But Benalmond was different. Although the Drummonds had moved out of it ninety years ago, it had been inhabited by tenants until the nineteen fifties, and since that time had been used by the Scouts, and briefly as a Youth Hostel. Unsuccessful attempts had been made to bring it into the nineteenth century, if not the twentieth. Many of the rooms had had their walls and ceilings plastered, and had fitments for gas lighting. Faded streamers of wallpaper fluttered from the walls. There was cracked brown linoleum on most of the floors, and forlorn, discarded pieces of furniture stood about, wardrobes, chests of drawers, sideboards crowned by spotted, yellowing mirrors. People had scrawled their names in pencil and felt pen on the plaster: 'Janet Rennick was here 1972', 'Peter loves Elise', 'Fudgie Rules OK'. Apart from the thickness of the walls, and the smallness of its windows, it was just like any other old, abandoned house; even the bathrooms were normal, if you allowed for mahogany casing around the bath-tubs, and blue roses on the veined enamel of the lavatory bowls.

'It doesn't feel like history,' complained Daisy to Bridget, as they wandered around a huge room on the second floor, one end of which was piled high with filthy mattresses and iron bedsteads from Benalmond's days as a Youth Hostel. But Bridget was not thinking of history. She was keeping a cold eye on Clementina, who once more was looking pale and weary and strangely old; you could see that she was doing her best to look interested, and talk brightly to Mrs Graham, but you knew that she was not enjoying herself at all.

Nothing unusual happened, however, until they had been all over the upper floors of the house, peeping into cupboards and glory-holes, and looking out of windows dizzily high above the tree-tops. They were descending, one behind the other, a spiral staircase on the opposite side of the house from the one where they had started, when Daisy, who was in front, said, 'Look! There's a passage here, with a little door at the end of it.'

'Let's have a peep,' said Bridget, who was just behind her.

They both side-stepped into a low-roofed tunnel, dim except for a gash of daylight under a sturdy but ill-fitting door. Daisy was just about to step forward and push it open, when she was aware of a commotion behind her. Beyond Bridget, she heard Mrs Graham say laughingly, 'Come on, then, kid. Hurry along. The passage is narrow, and I am wide . . .' then Clementina's voice, rising in a kind of frightened wail, 'No! No, please! Don't make me – I won't go in there, I can't. That's Charlie's room!'

There was an 'Ouch!' from Mrs Graham, as her bulk was squashed against the wall of the staircase by Clementina, struggling to get past. By the time Daisy and Bridget got out of the tunnel, Mrs Graham was sprawling on the steps, looking amazed, while all that remained of Clementina was the sound of her footsteps, pounding away down the stair, far below. By the time the other three had got themselves sorted out, and had caught up with her, she was sitting in the hall on a pile of broken wood, taking deep, sobbing breaths and shaking from head to foot.

Daisy and Bridget stood looking grave; they felt completely out of their depth. Mrs Graham, who was at her best when someone was distressed, went over to Clementina and held her firmly in her arms, talking to her very quietly, until at last her breathing became normal. Then she stood up, pushing her hair back from her face.

Bridget and Daisy heard Mrs Graham say, 'What's the matter, love? What frightened you?' and Clementina answer, 'I don't know. I don't know.'

'Well, never mind,' said Mrs Graham sensibly. 'I'm going to take you home and make you a cup of tea, then you must lie down for a while. Daisy and Bridget can take the key back to the Estate Office.'

Which they did, Daisy shocked and silent, Bridget speculating excitedly all the way. Who was Charlie, she wanted to know. When had Clementina been in that house before? What did she know that she wasn't telling?

Daisy did not know the answers to these questions. And, in the circumstances, she thought it would be wiser to keep to herself what she had heard in bed two nights before, when Clementina had seemed to be talking in her sleep.

'It wasn't the Redcoats, Angus. They didn't go back to the stables. It was Charlie. I know it was Charlie.'

7
The One-Day Trek

It could have been a very awkward evening. Clementina, at Mrs Graham's insistence, did go and lie down on her bed for a while, but she got up before supper and came downstairs, looking pale but perfectly composed. Bridget and Daisy, who had been warned by Mrs Graham that the incident in the Tower was on no account to be mentioned, responded with embarrassed noises to her apology.

'I'm sorry I was so silly, and upset you all. I don't know what came over me, really I don't.'

Supper was eaten mostly in silence, as Mrs Graham's topics of conversation, meeting with no response, fell like stones on to the ground.

But then, just as they were carrying their coffee out on to the verandah, Angus arrived, dressed in brown trousers and a clean striped shirt; he had come to find out why Clementina had not turned up at the Trekking Centre in the afternoon. He accepted Mrs Graham's offer of coffee, and sat down beside Clementina on a wicker sofa. They did not touch each other, or even exchange glances, but both Bridget and Daisy were rather achingly aware of the peace between them, and the relaxation in Clementina, because he was there. Bridget resented it. She was not pleased with Angus, and pretended to be absorbed in a paperback.

Mrs Graham, who was never in the least shy about quizzing people, now proceeded to quiz Angus, and, as always happened, he cheerfully told her everything she wanted to know. No, he said, he wasn't a local boy, exactly. His home was up at Balquhidder, where he lived with the Drummonds. This was a great surprise to Daisy and to Bridget, who pricked up her ears behind her book.

'My father was factor on the Drummond estates,' Angus said.

'He was what?' interrupted Daisy, who had never heard this word before.

'Factor,' repeated Angus. 'He's the man who looks after the estates for the owner – collects the rents, and makes sure that the property is kept in good condition. It's a very responsible job. Both my parents are dead,' he went on. 'They were drowned when their boat capsized on Loch Lubnaig in a thunderstorm, years ago, when I was only five. I was their only child, and I had no other family except for a granny in Strathyre who was too ill to look after me, so the Drummonds took me in. They've been marvellous to me, ever since – sent me to school with Mick, gave me a home in the holidays, and really treated me like a son. I'm here helping Mick for the summer, before I go to Agricultural College – after I graduate, I'm to factor the estates for Lord Drummond, like my father.'

'Then Mick is Lord Drummond's son,' said Daisy, thinking of the cheerful, friendly Mick who took them riding, and seemed so completely ordinary. 'I thought he was a groom.'

'Oh, no. He owns the Centre,' Angus told her. 'Quite a well-to-do lad is our Michael, but he can think of nothing but nags. When the Drummonds sold Benalmond to these Glasgow developers, it was part of the agreement that Mick should be allowed to run the horsey side of things. He's made a start with the pony-trekking, but he has plans for a stud farm, and a proper riding school.' He chuckled, and added, 'You must have seen him on television, at the Horse of the Year Show – Michael Drummond on Braes o' Balquhidder – doesn't that ring a bell? He's an awfu' lad for the cuddies, as the local folk say.'

'So you'll work for Mick, eventually?' Daisy asked. She was finding this fascinating.

'Oh, yes, I expect so,' Angus agreed. 'Not that his old dad is in any hurry to leave us, I'm glad to say. But of course I'll be Mick's factor one day, and I'll be proud of it. The Wisharts have always served the Drummonds. My grandfather was Mick's grandfather's adjutant in the First World War, and my father fought alongside Mick's father in the Second, when they were younger than Mick and I are now. And away back in the eighteenth century, my God-knows-how-many-greats-grandfather was body-servant to the Drummond who fought for the Stuarts at Culloden, and went into exile with him when the Cause was lost. I can't think of anything I'd rather be than Mick's factor, when the time comes. I'm a traditional kind of bloke.'

'Have some more coffee,' said Mrs Graham, 'and tell us where you and Mick went to school.'

They sat for ages in front of the chalet, drinking coffee while the summer night enfolded its darkness around them, and the brown moths came dancing suicidally around their lamp. Perhaps only Daisy noticed that Clementina's face was looking strained again; it had happened in an instant when Angus had told them about his ancestor's having been Lord Drummond's body-servant at the Battle of Culloden. It was half-past ten when Angus got up to go. He thanked Mrs Graham for the coffee, then, as if suddenly remembering, said, 'Listen. There's a one-day trek on Sunday. Why don't you all come? Mrs Graham?'

Mrs Graham laughed hilariously.

'My dear boy,' she said, 'I've no intention of getting my behind into a saddle at my advanced age. Pity the poor horse. The girls will come, though. I'm going out to lunch, and it will suit me nicely to get rid of them for a while.'

And so it was arranged.

Clementina went with Angus to the end of the track. She was not gone long, and when she came back she went straight upstairs to bed. Bridget was having a shower, so Daisy helped Mrs Graham to do the washing-up. She was used to being helpful in the house, and there was something she wanted to ask Mrs Graham, in private.

'Mrs – er, Harriet, I mean,' she said slowly, as she sorted out the cutlery and put it away in a drawer, 'what do you suppose was wrong with Clementina this afternoon?'

She did not usually approach things so directly, but this time she did not know how else to do it. And she desperately wanted some grown-up, sensible person to say that she was worried too.

Mrs Graham wiped the draining-board, and squeezed out the dishcloth.

'I've really no idea, Daisy,' she said. 'I have asked her, but I honestly don't think she knows either. She's just susceptible to atmosphere, I suppose. She's a terribly nervy creature, for all that she appears so self-possessed, and I dare say she's over-imaginative too. What do you think?'

Daisy saw at once that it was no use expecting anything more than this from Mrs Graham.

'I've no idea either,' she said hopelessly.

Sunday dawned clear and bright, with the morning sun drawing the outlines of the mountains razor sharp against the pale blue sky. There was not a cloud to be seen, and when the three girls set out from the chalet, carrying their packed lunches in small haversacks, the clean, sharp scent of the washed forest was so overwhelming that Daisy had one of those moments of pure delight, when she felt all through herself how marvellous it was to be Daisy Bradbrook, and thirteen years old. Even the burden of puzzled anxiety which she now carried around all the time could not spoil such a moment, although it settled down on her again gradually as they made their way through the wood, towards Benalmond Tower.

On the hour-long rides there were usually about twenty riders; today, however, there were obviously going to be fewer. Only five others were waiting outside the little office when the girls arrived, and only two more came after them. Presently the girl called Wendy came to take their money, and open up the little room where the hats and boots were kept. Meanwhile, Mick and Angus were leading out the ponies, already saddled, from their boxes, and turning them loose in the paddock, two by two. As soon as Clementina was ready, she went over the grass towards the pony, Billy. Billy came trotting eagerly, with a glad whinny of welcome, and stood pushing his nose into the crook of her elbow, and the palm of her hand.

'Hello, Gib. Hello, old fellow,' said Clementina, feeding him a lump of sugar, and fondling his dark, rough head.

Bridget watched them broodingly, as she and Daisy stood on the grass, waiting to have their ponies allocated.

'And that's another thing,' she said. 'She claims she's never ridden before, but have you noticed the way she handles that creature? You can see she's been riding for years – she's as good as Wendy, and nearly as good as Angus. Why does she have to tell lies about it?'

Daisy shook her head.

'I don't think she's telling lies, Bid,' she said. 'There'd be no point, as you say.'

'Well, how do you explain it, then?' enquired Bridget, not very pleasantly.

'I don't,' admitted Daisy.

She watched Clementina spring lightly into the saddle, gathering up the reins in confident hands. The horse danced playfully under her, and she laughed as she brought him under control, and let him canter a little up and down the paddock. It was true that no novice ever rode like Clementina, yet Daisy did not believe that she was telling lies. The mystery was deeper than that.

Angus came, and held the ponies while Daisy and Bridget heaved themselves on to their backs. Once they were up, it was not so bad, but so far they had failed to achieve that easy leap to the saddle which they so envied in Clementina.

'Well done, Stiffy,' said Angus to Bridget, earning himself yet another black mark.

Daisy was pleased to find herself on Tam again; he was a nice little pony with a wise, funny face. Bridget had Tinker, but would have preferred Coxy. Last time she had had Coxy, but would have preferred Tinker.

'Now, listen, boys and girls,' said Mick, who was mounted on a rather handsome grey called Knight, 'and I'll tell you what we're going to do. The plan is to go up the side of the Duchray Water to Blairvaich, then strike north through the forest to the side of Loch Ard, where we'll have lunch. In the afternoon we'll ride round the loch to the waterfall at Ledard, and be back here between four and five. I'll go in front with Wendy, and Angus will bring up the rear. No one is to pass me, please, or get behind Angus. Otherwise you may ride in any formation you like.'

It was at this point that Daisy noticed a peculiar

expression of bright interest on Bridget's face, but, for the moment, its significance escaped her – mercifully, because, if she had guessed at nine o'clock in the morning what Bridget was up to, it would have ruined the whole of her day, instead of only half of it.

A ride through the forest on such a perfect summer morning was full of delights, with a clear little river talking busily to itself beside you, and all around the soldierly ranks of fir and pine, thrown into disarray here and there by outbursts of oak and birch. Tam knew the way better than Daisy did, so she was able to relax, and listen, and appreciate things. Once she saw a red squirrel, clinging with its minute hands to the bark of a pine tree, and down by the water there were sandpipers, and dippers, and beautiful black and white oyster-catchers, which before now she had only seen in her father's bird books. From far away in the valley, the clear sound of a church bell was lifted up to them; it reminded Daisy of what she would normally be doing at this time on a Sunday morning, and she was glad that she had home to go back to when all this was over. Presently she had a pleasant chat to a boy and girl who were on holiday from Staffordshire; they were staying at a hotel in Aberfoyle, and had heard about the pony-trekking from Angus, who had been in the village having his hair cut.

They had been riding for more than an hour before Daisy even noticed that Bridget had deserted her. Looking up ahead, she saw that her friend was now riding with Wendy and Mick. Getting in with the show-jumping set, thought Daisy, laughing to herself as Tam picked his way through a little stream that ran across their path. It was lunch-time before she realised that it was no laughing matter.

They stopped to have their picnic by a little tree-ringed bay on the shore of Loch Ard. The ponies were turned loose on a patch of grass, and Angus and Wendy brought them water from a cottage near the loch side. The trekkers arranged themselves in groups to eat their packed lunches, some down on the stony shore by the water, others further up, in the shade of the trees. It was now very hot, without a whisper of a breeze. Daisy sat down with Katie and Paul, the pair from Staffordshire, and waited for Bridget to join her. She had finished her slice of pork pie, and was about to start on her egg sandwiches, before it dawned on her that Bridget had no intention of doing any such thing.

Angus and Clementina, Wendy and Mick had sat down together some distance away from where Daisy was. Now Daisy realised with horror that Bridget had gatecrashed their picnic, and was making the most obvious attempt to gain the attention of Mick Drummond. Daisy was too far away to hear a word Bridget was saying, but what she had in mind was all too easy to guess. She was gesticulating and smiling into Mick's face, asking him to open her can of lemonade, squealing and pretending to be afraid of creepy-crawlies, so that he was obliged by good manners to lean over and remove some innocent earwig which had climbed on to her cardigan. Daisy watched in pained disbelief. First Angus, now Mick. She was only thankful that Clementina had her back turned towards her, so that she could not catch her eye.

On the ride round the loch in the afternoon, Bridget was just as awful. It was a ride on road, and Mick had told them that they must stay in single file. Somehow, Bridget had managed to push Tinker in between Mick and Wendy; Daisy could see her head nodding as she chattered away up in front, to Mick's unresponsive back.

It would not have been quite so distressing, Daisy thought, if Bridget had not said, over and over again, how dull and plain Mick was, with his broad, brown face, small, greenish eyes and untidy, lustreless black hair. But that was when she had thought he was only a groom.

The afternoon was as beautiful as the morning had been, the loch as blue and the purple mountains as majestic, but for Daisy the colour had gone out of everything. She was angry and humiliated because of Bridget's behaviour, and spent most of the ride back steeling herself, for once, to give Bridget a large piece of her mind. Then why, she wondered bitterly, did her feelings have to be complicated, at the last minute, by a profound pity for Bridget? For it is never pleasant to see a friend hurt; now Bridget was hurt, and it was no help to say she had thoroughly deserved it.

When they got back to the Trekking Centre, just on five o'clock, Daisy watched Bridget dismount, and say goodbye effusively to Mick – no doubt telling him what a wonderful day she had had. Mick said goodbye shortly, but perfectly pleasantly, and began to lead Knight and Tinker away to their stable, and their evening meal. Bridget turned, and as if noticing Daisy for the first time, came smiling over the grass to where she was standing with Angus and Clementina.

'What a nice boy Mick is,' she began. 'I hadn't realised —' but Angus, without any display of his own feelings, cut her short.

'Look, kid,' he said. 'You're as well to know. You really needn't bother. He's engaged to Wendy Robertson, and they're only waiting until he's twenty-one before they marry. They've known each other since they were in their prams.'

8
A Change of Tune

The following day, for the first time, Daisy felt that she simply had to get away from Bridget for a while. Although she had lived for as long as she could remember in a house overrun by children – her youngest brother, Ben, was still barely three – she had always, as the eldest, had a room of her own where she could go, and shut the door, and be by herself for a little. The most stressful thing about living in the chalet at Benalmond was that the nearest you ever got to privacy was going to the loo, or lying in bed with your face to the wall. Otherwise you were surrounded all the time by people who didn't get on, so that the air seemed to twang with vibrations of anger. It was very tiring. So next morning, when Clementina was sawing away at her discordant sonata, and Bridget was washing her underwear, Daisy slipped out of the house without telling anyone she was going. She would walk to Aberfoyle, she decided, buy some toothpaste and shampoo, and walk back again. If she missed lunch, Mrs Graham wouldn't care, and by this time, neither did she.

It was another misty morning, but of the kind which Daisy now knew held promise of a brighter afternoon. Meanwhile, she enjoyed the coolness, as she walked along the verge of the narrow road, looking at the wild flowers, and listening to the busy rustlings of unseen dwellers in the ditch. She scuffled her feet in the whinstone chips which the traffic had pushed to the side of the road, and for the first mile or so managed to keep her mind away from the troubles which seemed to be closing in around her. But after that they all came flooding back, the memory of yesterday most painfully. The result of that disaster was that Bridget was now in a huff with everyone; most unfairly, she seemed to blame both Daisy and Clementina for her humiliation. It was not a pleasant prospect, two more weeks as the guest of someone who had stopped talking to you. And then there was Clementina herself, beautiful, silent and unwilling to share either her thoughts or her company with anyone at the chalet. It was unthinkable to Daisy that she might tackle Clementina about the strangeness of her behaviour: for one thing, it would be inviting a dreadful snub, and for another, it would be admitting the possibility of something which she did not want to think about. Daisy felt, in her confused way, that if she began to put her fears and suspicions about Clementina into words, putting them into words would make them come true. Instead, she repeated to herself all the things which Mrs Graham had said; Clementina was sensitive, over-imaginative, nervy. But did that explain why she rode a wild horse like a professional, how she knew things that she ought not to have known? Angrily, Daisy ordered herself to stop being a fool. She rode the horse as she did because she was what was called a born rider, and she knew what she did because she had read it in a book in her school library. Everyone did a project about the Jacobites at some time. And as for the fact that Clementina's surname was the same as that of a long ago Lady Drummond – that was coincidental, for Heaven's sake. It was a common enough name, Rattray. There were dozens of them in the telephone directory. Daisy had looked. But she knew that as an explanation, it wouldn't do at all.

She crossed a bridge, and walked on towards the village.

The long grey main street of Aberfoyle was crowded with tourists, cyclists and hikers and caravanners in summer shirts, buying Coke and Edinburgh rock and tartan souvenirs from gift shops which displayed their hideous wares in every second window. Daisy bought her shampoo and toothpaste at a chemist's, treated herself to an iced lolly, and set off on the road back to Benalmond.

But on this stage of her journey she had not gone half a mile before she had had enough. Her legs were slightly stiff, and her bottom slightly sore from yesterday's ride, and soon she was hoping against hope that the blue country bus would come along, so that she could have a ride home. But the buses on that route were very infrequent, and indeed there was little traffic of any kind. In the end it was not the sound of an engine, but the stately clip-clop of hoofs that she heard behind her. Glancing over her shoulder, she saw Mick Drummond, riding Knight, coming along the road.

Daisy could not think of anyone she was less anxious to meet. On the rides, Mick had been friendly to her in a casual, teasing kind of way; he had made rude remarks about her short legs, and pointed out to Angus that she and Tam looked exactly like a Thelwell cartoon. Daisy, who had brothers, was used to this sort of cheek from boys, so she did not flounce, as Bridget would have done, making them laugh all the more. Ordinarily she wouldn't have minded a bit of teasing from Mick in passing, but after yesterday .... She wondered whether it would be possible to melt into the wood, and skulk there till he had gone past, but when she slewed her eyes to the right, she saw that a wide, overgrown ditch and a barbed wire fence would have to be negotiated before she reached the shelter of the plantation. There simply wasn't time. She was trying to decide whether she should wave, or say, 'Good morning', or keep her head down, and say nothing, when the horse's long grey legs came abreast of her, and, to her astonishment, halted. She looked up a long way, and saw Mick's weather-beaten face grinning down at her.

'Morning, Shorty,' he said. 'You look as if your little legs are weary. Do you want a lift?'

'It's very kind of you,' said Daisy, swallowing hard.

'OK. Get up on the verge, and give me your hand,' ordered Mick. 'Now, put your toe on my foot. That's it.'

And before she knew what was happening, Daisy was sitting astride Knight's shining neck, with Mick's tweed-sleeved arms fencing her in securely on either side. He touched the horse with his knees, made a clicking sound with his tongue, and Knight moved forward, carrying two as easily as one.

Mick did not talk, and neither did Daisy; she found that you could be silent with Mick and not feel awkward at all. She sat with her hands lightly on Knight's silky mane, enjoying the horse's movement and the warmth of his body on the insides of her legs. All too soon they came to the unicorn gates of Benalmond, and Mick said, 'Do you mind if I put you down here? I'm going on to see someone at Kinlochard.'

Daisy said, 'Thank you. Not at all,' and got down the way she had come up.

But then, greatly to her surprise, Mick dismounted too, and stood beside her, holding Knight's head, and looking down at her from a height of over six feet.

'Listen,' he said. 'Daisy, isn't it? This is really no business of mine, but is there something the matter? You looked all in when I met you back there, and all day yesterday you were perfectly miserable. Nobody should look like that at your age.'

Daisy was astounded. Astounded that Mick should even have noticed how she looked, even more astounded that he should take the trouble to ask why. She felt herself going scarlet to the roots of her spiky brown hair, and she could not think how to reply.

'If you're bothering about your friend, you know,' Mick went on, 'you don't have to. Maybe she's bowled over by my handsome face, but I think it's more likely she's feeling lonely, and would just like to have a boy-friend. Only, you see, I'm booked – and I'm far too old for her, anyway.'

'Yes,' Daisy said. 'I know. Oh, it's partly that, and partly – it isn't anything I can talk about properly, Mick. It has just been a rotten holiday, and we had looked forward to it so much. I hadn't realised how little you know people, until you have to share a bedroom with them.'

Mick laughed then, his face splitting into a vast grin.

'It's obvious you've never been to boarding-school,' he said, 'if you've reached thirteen without learning that. However, don't despair. Holidays do come to an end. And remember, if you ever want someone to talk to, I'm up at the stables.'

With which he mounted Knight, saluted her with his riding crop, and rode away along the road.

In a haze of hero-worship, Daisy turned in between the unicorns, and walked up the drive. Whoever would have believed it, she kept saying to herself. Of course, she would never dream of going up to the stables, and unburdening herself to Mick – but it was a comfort to know that one person, among all those she had met at Benalmond, noticed how other people were looking, and cared. As she opened the chalet door, it occurred to Daisy to wonder what Mick Drummond thought about Clementina.

When Daisy went upstairs, Clementina was still practising her music in Mrs Graham's room. It was obvious how Clementina intended to get through the rest of the holiday. She would either be closeted in the only private place in the house, playing her violin, or she would be up at the Trekking Centre with Angus, and her beloved Gib. Daisy could not help feeling a little bitter. It was all very well for Clementina, who was not Bridget's guest, tied to Bridget by the demands of a friendship which was wearing sadly thin. It was wonderfully easy to be Mrs Graham's guest, for that entailed no responsibility at all. But no sooner had Daisy thought this than she felt ashamed. She would not have cared to change places with Clementina.

Daisy had expected to find Bridget in their room, sulking. So it was a relief to find the room empty, and be able to lie on her bed, and feel the warmth of the sun, which had now penetrated the mists of morning, falling through the window across her feet. Daisy lay for a while, thinking of Mick Drummond, and only gradually did the awareness seep into her mind that Clementina, next door, had changed her tune. Daisy had never heard her playing that sort of music before. She kept her eyes shut, and listened.

Clementina, it seemed, had grown tired of the discords of her Bulgarian composer, and she had begun to improvise on an old Scots tune, which Daisy recognised as one which Angus was always whistling and singing as he went about his work, *'O whistle, and I'll come to you, my lad'*. But before Daisy even had time to start fitting in the words, Clementina had drawn that melody away into others, which Daisy knew were the songs of the Jacobites; she knew them, but Clementina's weaving of them was so elusive that one moment the tune was there, the next it had become something else. Not that Daisy cared. It was lovely to lie there drowsy in the sunshine, lapped about by beautiful sounds. Then suddenly, a whole song came through.

'I swear by moon and stars sae bright,
And sun that glances early,
If I had twenty thousand lives,
I'd gie them a' for Charlie.
We'll o'er the water,
We'll o'er the sea,
We'll o'er the water to Charlie;
Come weel, come wo,
We'll gather and go,
And live or die wi' Charlie.'

Charlie again, Daisy mused. Charlie's room. Prince Charlie. Was it possible that Benalmond was one of the many houses, great and small, that had been proud and eager to offer a night's lodging to that dear and dangerous guest? And if so, how should Clementina know, and why should she care? But as usual, she could only think of the questions, not the answers.

Just then the door opened, and Clementina appeared, carrying her violin case and some music, which she proceeded to stow away in the wardrobe.

'Hello,' she said to Daisy. 'I didn't hear you come in. Where've you been?'

'Aberfoyle. I needed shampoo,' said Daisy. She sat up, felt about for her shoes, and added, 'I liked that. What you were playing, I mean.'

Clementina turned from the dressing-table, where she was combing her hair, and gave Daisy a grimace of surprise.

'Did you?' she asked. 'You must have advanced taste. I can't stand it myself, and as for what Harriet and Bridget think – it doesn't bear repeating. However, keep calm – I'll be back on Brahms tomorrow.'

Daisy buckled her sandals, and straightened up.

'No, no,' she said. 'That's not what I mean. I mean what you were playing a few minutes ago. The Scottish tunes.'

Clementina was standing opposite her, so that Daisy could see her face clearly. And she would have sworn that Clementina's blank look was genuine, her bewilderment honest. For a moment, Daisy thought she was going to be angry, but then she laughed, and tried to pass the matter off as a joke.

'Scottish tunes?' she said. 'That's the first time I've ever heard old Mousy Cheese Cheek's stuff described so nicely. It doesn't sound like Scottish tunes to me. Now come on – let's see what's for lunch. I'm starving, and so must you be, after such a long walk.'

And with the air of one humouring an idiot, she led the way downstairs.

9
Letters on Glass

It was all very confusing, but Daisy had not much time to think, since, for the rest of the day, she was busy helping Mrs Graham to put a mountain of her lecture notes in order – a frustrating task, but better than the alternative, which was going with Bridget to the golf-course. By evening, the incident of the music had taken its place in Daisy's mind as just one more inexplicable part of the mystery which was Clementina. She did not even brood about it much when she was in bed, because she was too busy screwing up her courage to tackle Bridget about the terrible way their friendship was falling apart. She was scared, because she thought Bridget was likely to fly off the handle and make a scene, but she told herself sternly that two more weeks of huff would be much worse than a quick row to clear the air.

So, as soon as she had tidied the bedroom next morning, and watched from the window Clementina hurrying along the sun-dappled path on her way to Angus, Daisy went downstairs to where Bridget was sitting on the back doorstep, reading a magazine.

'Push along,' said Daisy, and when Bridget reluctantly did so, squeezed herself into the narrow space between Bridget's shoulder and the doorpost. Really, she reflected, all this rich food was making Bridget enormous – but this was hardly the time to mention it. So she took a deep breath and went on, 'Now, listen, Bid, please. This has got to stop, you know.'

Predictably, Bridget's hackles rose.

'And what has got to stop, may I enquire?' she demanded haughtily.

'Yes, you may,' returned Daisy. It was not so difficult, she found, after a start had been made. 'And I shall tell you. You have got to stop behaving as if I'm to blame for everything that has annoyed you about this holiday. Because I'm not. I've been friendly, and I've taken your side —' she did not add, 'even when you've been completely in the wrong,' although she was tempted to do so '— and I don't see any reason why you should be in the huff with me.'

'You laughed at that tasteless joke of Mother's about the crutches,' said Bridget stiffly.

'I can't help laughing at your mother. It's the effect she has on me,' explained Daisy, smothering the inclination to laugh again. 'However, I'm sorry if I hurt your feelings. The point is, I'm your friend, and you should realise that, and stop being so snappy.'

There was a long pause, while Bridget stared at her. Daisy thought she might be going to hit her, or get up and stalk away with her nose in the air. But she didn't. She sighed, leaned back against the doorpost, and said, 'You're quite right, Dais. It isn't your fault. I'm just in such a rage about that awful girl. She's ruined everything we'd planned.'

Daisy did not attempt to argue about this. There was no point in trying to reason with someone so completely unreasonable. She just felt relieved that Bridget was proving reasonable on the point which mattered most to her.

'Look, Bid,' she said earnestly, 'whatever other people do, you and I can still have some fun during the time that's left here. Let's try to forget Angus and Clementina – we need hardly ever see them, after all.'

It was wise advice, and, for a little while, it seemed as if Bridget had heeded it. She and Daisy went to the swimming-pool, and enjoyed a lovely cool swim; afterwards they lay on the pool side, drinking orange juice and munching potato crisps. And Daisy thought it was just like the old days at home, when Bridget was her best friend, and she really scarcely knew her.

On the way back, however, it became clear that Bridget would not so easily forget her obsession with Clementina. Perhaps she was reminded of her grievances by the sight of Clementina riding Gib up the drive, with Angus at her side, or perhaps it was that she simply could not keep Clementina out of her thoughts for long. Whatever was the truth, as she came along the shore with Daisy, she said, 'I've been thinking, Dais. I'd really like to have another look at that room in the Tower – the one there was all the fuss about, you know. I didn't even have time to glance at it, before the rumpus began, and it's just possible that it holds some clue to – well, to whatever's going on. I think she didn't want us to go in, and all that kerfuffle was to create a diversion.'

Daisy remembered the sobbing, shaking figure sitting among the debris in the hall, and wanted to point out that Clementina would have had to be a professional actress to stage a diversion like that. But she did not want to be accused of being unco-operative, so soon after peace had been declared, so instead she said, 'I expect it's quite an ordinary room – the rest of the place was a bit disappointing, didn't you think? And anyway, how would we get in? The work seems to have stopped again, and the place is all locked up.'

'Oh, I'll ask for the key at the Estate Office,' said Bridget airily. 'I'll say it's all right by Mr Briggs.'

'Well – I think – if you're really terribly keen to go in again – it would be better to get permission properly through your mother,' advised Daisy. 'It's a private place, and if we were caught trespassing, there might be an awful row.'

'Oh, all right, then,' said Bridget, who was in a good mood with Daisy. 'Since you're so fussy, I'll do it legally. Mother will be able to get us a key from her pal Briggs, no doubt.'

Daisy left it at that, although she did notice that Bridget, who was so censorious about Clementina, was not above telling the odd lie herself, to get what she wanted.

Mrs Graham was in the sitting-room when they got back, crawling about on the floor, rearranging the papers which Daisy had arranged yesterday, and marking the bundles illegibly with red biro. She sat back on her heels when the girls came in, pushing wisps of fair hair out of her eyes, and comically blowing out her flushed round cheeks.

'This is plan B,' she said. 'Sorry, Daisy.'

Bridget picked her way through white drifts to an armchair, flopped into it, and proceeded to give her mother a version of what she had in mind.

'We really didn't manage to see everything the last time, because of what happened,' she said, 'and it was so fascinating. Daisy and I thought we'd like to have another look round. Can you arrange it for us, Mother?'

Mrs Graham, who had forgotten that Bridget had not seemed unduly fascinated on their last visit, was only too willing to help. She had a genuine desire to see her young people happy.

'Of course, darling,' she said easily. 'We'll ask Jerry. Actually, he's coming round for a pre-lunch drink, so it couldn't be more convenient. Only this time we'll have to convince him that you can look after yourselves – I'm much too busy to come with you again. And I do think it would be wiser not to take Clementina.'

'I wasn't thinking of it,' said Bridget, rolling her eyes

ceilingwards. When they had gone out on to the verandah to hang their wet swimming things on the railing, Daisy remarked, 'How exciting. I'm all agog to see your Mum's new boy-friend.'

Bridget sighed.

'Oh dear,' she said. 'I do hope she's not serious. She's forty-three, for Heaven's sake. You'd think she'd have more sense at that age, wouldn't you?'

'If she marries him, your name will be Bridget Briggs,' Daisy could not resist telling her, and got a wet swim-suit in her face as a reply.

When Mr Briggs arrived, however, it was clear that Bridget was not in immediate danger of acquiring a stepfather. He was a large, grey-haired widower of sixty, who chatted about his grown-up daughters and his grandchildren. Watching like hawks, Bridget and Daisy could see nothing romantic in the way he and Mrs Graham behaved to each other. It occurred to Daisy that perhaps Mrs Graham was just glad to have another grown-up to talk to, after a fortnight with teenage girls.

Yes, Mr Briggs said, he would arrange for them to have a key again, as long as they promised to be careful, and not touch any of the workmen's tools and materials. It was unlikely, he told them, that any more work would be done on the reconstruction till September, as the men were now working on a job at Lochgilphead, which had to be finished to fulfil a contract.

'Just be careful that you don't disturb the ghost,' he warned them, laughing, as he finished his whisky and soda, and stood up to leave.

'What ghost?' demanded Bridget eagerly. 'I didn't know there was a ghost.'

'Oh, every place that old in Scotland has a ghost,' said Mr Briggs. 'They're all bloody towers, when it comes to it. This one was a poor relation – or was she a governess? I can't remember. Anyway, she and the young lady of the house were both in love with the same man – he was a coachman, I think, or maybe a gamekeeper. And when he unwisely showed that he favoured the governess, if that's what she was, the young lady did him in. Whereupon the governess died of grief, or smallpox, or something, and now flits about on moonlit nights, wailing – oh well, you know the form.'

'You don't seem a hundred per cent sure of your facts, Jerry,' said Mrs Graham, much amused.

'But how?' Daisy wanted to know. 'Did she do him in, I mean?'

'I've no idea. I heard the story from Mrs MacAlister, who runs the cafeteria, and is an expert on the Drummonds, self-styled. I don't think she was a hundred per cent sure of her facts either. Do you believe in ghosts, Miss Bradbrook?'

'I keep an open mind,' said Daisy.

'And I keep a closed one,' replied Mr Briggs. 'Well, I must be off. Many thanks for the drink, Harriet. See you on Thursday?'

Daisy was more reluctant than ever to go into the Tower again, now that she thought she might meet a ghost, but Bridget, whose mind was as closed to such possibilities as Mr Briggs's was, was determined to have her way.

'You don't have to go to any of the spooky rooms we were in before,' she pointed out, as patiently as she could in the face of Daisy's silliness. 'I only want to see that one room. Besides, your ghost only comes out on moonlit nights, and we're going in the afternoon.'

'Very comforting,' said Daisy.

But, because she did not want to fall out with Bridget, so soon after falling in, she went with her to fetch the key, and accompanied her to the Tower.

As the door swung shut behind them, cutting off at a stroke the bright liveliness of the outdoor summer day, the silence of that vast, empty place seemed to press down on them from the five floors above. The now familiar, rubbly smell seeped into their noses, and Daisy shivered, only partly on account of the sudden cold. But Bridget said, 'Come on, then – no point in wasting time,' and shone her torch in the direction of the left-hand archway. Daisy followed her down the passage and up the spiral staircase, its sandstone steps worn to half their original depth by the passage of generations of feet. They found the little passage leading off to the left, two and a half floors up, and, with a nervous sense of expectation, pushed open the heavy oak door at the end of it. It swung back a little reluctantly on dry hinges.

But the room was a disappointment, to Bridget at least, because it was empty. It had a feeling of oldness, compared with the rooms they had seen on their last visit, because its walls had never been plastered, and its dusty floor was not covered in tattered linoleum. There were no cupboards, no chests of drawers for Bridget to pry into, but nonetheless she fussed around, running her fingers over the walls, poking into cracks with a pencil, knocking on wood. While Daisy waited, she wandered over to the small, deep-set window, and with a paper tissue tried to wipe away the grime and cobwebs which covered its square grey panes. Startled spiders scuttled angrily away. Daisy had hoped for a view, but the window was filled with beech leaves, and she could see nothing beyond. But she did see something within. In a corner of the bottom right hand pane, standing out frostily against the glass, were some letters and figures enclosed in a ring. Daisy knew that you could get this effect by scratching glass with a diamond. There were two sets of initials, 'CD' on top of 'AW', and underneath a date, 1745. Daisy stared for a long time, but she did not call Bridget over to share her discovery. The days were now long past when she got pleasure from sharing anything at all with Bridget.

In the evening, when Bridget was washing her hair, and she had a blessed half-hour of her own, Daisy went down to the shore to practise her stone-skimming. And there it occurred to her that the initials she had seen on the window were, in fact, familiar. 'AW' might have stood for Angus Wishart, and 'CD' for Clementina – but no. Of course not. That was silly. Clementina's name was Rattray, and the initial 'D', in that house, obviously stood for Drummond. And anyway, she reminded herself crossly, as stone after stone plopped straight down into the water, the date was 1745, and Angus and Clementina were now. How could there be any connection? Clementina's Rattrays had been fishmongers in Dundee, and only the coincidence of the shared surname bound her to the Drummonds of Benalmond at all. Which would have been a more comforting thought had Daisy not discovered, a little later that same evening, that it was not strictly true.

It was growing chilly on the shore, and to divert her mind, Daisy decided that she would go upstairs, fetch paper and pencil, and make a list of the presents she was going to buy to take home to her family. Would her father like a new fountain-pen, she wondered, for writing his sermons, and would her little sisters like clothes-peg dollies dressed as a Highland chief, or Mary, Queen of Scots? Occupied with these thoughts, she climbed the stair and went into the bedroom, which was deserted; Bridget had gone down to the sitting-room to watch a film on television, and Clementina had not yet returned from the Trekking Centre.

As usual, Bridget's corner of the room was chaotic, with discarded clothes all over the bed and chair, and on the floor a wild strewing of books, papers, jars, tissues and brushes. Clementina's corner was tidy, but, as she entered, Daisy noticed that a book had slipped from the bed on to the floor, and that a sheet of paper had fallen out of it. Automatically she stepped forward and picked up the book, then the paper. At first she thought it was a loose page, and glanced down to see the number, so that she could put it back in its correct place. But then she saw that it was not that sort of paper at all.

It was an application form for a student grant at St Cecilia's College of Music, Chiswick, and with widening eyes Daisy read what Clementina had printed on it.

Surname: RATTRAY

Christian or forenames: CLEMENTINA ARABEL

Name and Occupation of father:
DRUMMOND CHARLES RATTRAY
JOURNALIST (deceased)

Probably Daisy had heard Clementina's step on the stair, but she had been too shocked to react. So she had a sense of being taken by surprise when the lock clicked, the door opened, and Clementina stood there, looking normal in her blue jeans and green anorak. Her eyes met Daisy's in a long, expressionless stare.

It was Daisy who spoke first. Slowly she folded the paper and handed it to Clementina, saying, 'If I were you, I'd put this away somewhere safe. Anyone might pick it up, and you know how some people do carry on.'

Relief flooded Clementina's pale face, and tears came into her eyes.

'Thanks, Daisy,' was all she said, as, folding the paper over and over until it was very small, she went to lock it away in her violin case.

Daisy busied herself looking for a pencil and her

writing-pad, although for the life of her she couldn't remember what she had intended to do with them. When she turned around, Clementina had closed the wardrobe door, and was looking at her with frightened, pleading eyes.

'It's coincidence,' she said. 'Only coincidence, Daisy. You do believe that, don't you?'

'Of course,' said Daisy.

She could not think of anything else to say.

10
A Supper Party

Coincidence. Of course it was coincidence. Daisy told herself so a hundred times during a sleepless night, and a hundred times more during the next day, as she picnicked in the forest with Bridget and her friends the Morrisons. And sometimes she almost believed that it was true. But why, if it were all a matter of coincidence – that serviceable, feeble word we use to ward off any uncomfortable thing which we cannot explain – should she be overwhelmed by this desolating feeling that something terrible was going to happen, and that nothing could be done to avoid it? She kept remembering the expression in Clementina's eyes when she turned round from the wardrobe, and wondering whether she knew it too. To tell yourself over and over that it was all coincidence, and that this ghastly holiday had got you into a bad nervous state, was the only defence against such feelings, and Daisy clung to it in desperation. Ten more days, not counting today, she kept telling herself. Just let me get safely through ten more days, and I need never think about the Drummonds of Benalmond again, as long as I live.

Daisy did not see Clementina again until the evening. She had spent so much of the last twenty-four hours having nightmarish thoughts about her that it was quite a surprise to see Clementina looking ordinary, and hear her having a normal conversation with Mrs Graham across the supper-table. You had to admire her coolness, Daisy thought.

'Harriet, dear, are you in the mood to do me a favour?'

'I don't know. You had better try me out,' said Mrs Graham.

'Well, it's like this,' went on Clementina. 'You know how I've spent such a lot of time up at the stables, and they've been so decent, never charging me for riding Gib, and letting me share their grub at lunch-time. And now Mick has even promised to take Gib up to his parents' place at Balquhidder, so that I can ride him there when I visit – on other holidays, you know. I feel I'd like to do something in return. I can't afford to take them to a hotel, or anything like that, so I wondered – would you let me invite them here to supper one evening? There would be Angus, and Mick and Wendy, and Wendy's cousin Winnie, who has just arrived from London. Is it awful cheek of me to ask, Harriet?'

'Not at all, my dear,' replied Mrs Graham warmly. 'It's a nice idea, and of course I'll be delighted to help. Now, I wonder – what shall we have to eat?'

Paying no attention at all to the scowl on Bridget's face, she launched happily into a catalogue of all the delicious things she could cook.

'Oysters are out,' she said regretfully. 'And salmon – no, I don't think we'll have that. They'll get so much of it that it will just be like kippers to an Aberdonian. I know – I'll make *coq au vin* for the main course – I'm a wizard at *coq au vin*, amn't I, Biddy? And how about avocado mousse for the starter – or my leeks *vinaigrette*? Not corn on the cob, I think – it's too embarrassing when all the butter runs down your chin and drips on to your bosom. Well, my bosom, anyway. What do you think?'

Clementina said hastily that avocado mousse would be lovely, and please, could they have trifle for pudding, because it was Angus's favourite?

'I make a wonderful trifle,' Mrs Graham assured her. 'Awash with sherry, and smothered in whipped cream. Raspberry or lime for the jelly, dear? It's all one to me.'

Usually, Daisy found this sort of performance by Mrs Graham very funny. But tonight she was not amused. Suddenly, there was no room in her heart for any feeling but envy, envy of someone who had been invited to stay at Mick Drummond's house in the holidays.

On the morning of the party, however, she offered to help Mrs Graham in the kitchen. She liked cooking, and thought that perhaps it might keep her thoughts from other things. She was still counting the days till the holiday would be over, and they would all be safely home; only eight to go now, and with any luck, three of these would be spent away at Loch Lomond on the pony-trek. She had a peculiar idea that out of doors was safer, away from buildings; more sensibly she reckoned that it would be easier to steer clear of both Bridget and Clementina in a crowd of ordinary young people. She mentioned the camp while they were all having a quick soup-and-cheese lunch on the verandah. Later, she was to wish bitterly that she had held her tongue.

'I've been thinking,' she said, 'that if we're going on a three-day trek, it will have to be the next one, won't it? I mean, a week on Sunday, we'll all be going home.'

She hoped that she did not sound as eager and pleased as she felt when she said this, but if she did, no one seemed to notice.

'You're right,' said Mrs Graham through a mouthful of Camembert and slimmers' Ryvita. 'When does the next camp start, does anyone know?'

'Monday,' said Clementina. 'It's usually Wednesday, but it's being brought forward, because it's Mick's twenty-first birthday next Saturday, and he needs time to get ready for his party. So the camp's Monday to Wednesday next week.'

'Fine,' said Mrs Graham, with a note of satisfaction in her voice. 'Make sure you put your names down, girls.'

Then Bridget put down her plate, and stretched out with self-conscious nonchalance on her chair.

'Oh, I meant to tell you, but I forgot,' she said lightly. 'I've changed my mind, actually. I don't think pony-trekking is quite me.'

It was generally agreed that Mrs Graham was the most placid of women. But, as is true of many easy-going people, on the odd occasion when she did lose her temper, her performance was spectacular. She lost her temper now. Clementina and Daisy watched in fascination as the pink of her round cheeks deepened to scarlet, her mild blue eyes narrowed to glinting slits, and her fat body shook with rage. Bridget cowered before the coming storm.

'Listen you,' bawled her mother, completely ignoring their neighbours, who were also lunching on their verandahs. 'You'll damn well go if I say so, see? I've been cooped up in this flaming hut for three weeks with bloody kids, and now when I do get the chance of three days' peace and quiet, Madam has decided that pony-trekking isn't quite her. What is you, for God's sake? Well, you're going, and if you get blisters on your behind, tough luck. I'm not going to be done out of three days when I don't have to see your sour face every time I turn round —'

At this point, Clementina gave a loud snort of laughter, and fled. Daisy gave a loud, exploding snort of laughter, and followed her. Afterwards, she could never think why she did, because she did not really think it was funny; she was shocked rigid by being called a bloody kid. And she knew that the damage would never be repaired. Bridget could not bear to be laughed at, and Daisy knew that neither she nor Clementina would ever be forgiven.

Surprisingly, after all this, the party was a great success. Mick and Angus, Wendy and Winnie seemed pleased to be invited to what Wendy called a civilised meal. Mrs Graham had laid on lots of white wine – 'Fortified lemonade, darling,' she said airily to Daisy as she filled her glass for the third time – and soon even Daisy was chattering merrily. Bridget was being pleasant, and polite, but Daisy was too busy to find this as ominous as she normally would have done. Mrs Graham, quite recovered from her fit of temper, presided in a flutter of pink ruffles. Mick and Angus complimented her fulsomely on her cooking, and flirted with her, which she loved. Clementina sat beside Angus, not talking very much, but obviously pleased that the party was going so well.

When they had finished the trifle and eaten most of the cheese, they took their coffee into the sitting-room.

'Awful, isn't it?' said Mrs Graham hilariously, as she switched on the lamp and fell into a gigantic armchair. 'I always feel as if I ought to be mowing the carpet in here. It will be quite a relief to get back to slum conditions next week-end.'

'Next week-end?' repeated Mick, who had settled himself on the sheepskin hearthrug with his coffee on his lap. 'Are you really going home next week-end? Which day?'

'Sunday,' said Mrs Graham, fishing about in her bag for her cigarettes. 'I don't suppose any of you smoke, do you?' she asked. 'Well, I shall, if you don't mind, since it's a party. Yes, Sunday,' she went on. 'I can't say I'll be sorry.'

'Oh, that's all right, then,' said Mick, looking relieved. 'You see, it's my twenty-first birthday on Saturday, and we're having a party. You're all invited, of course.'

'How very kind,' said Mrs Graham graciously. 'The girls will be delighted, won't you girls? But I don't think I should come, Mick, nice though it is of you to ask me. Unless you're having a separate grannies' section, that is.'

'Oh, but we are,' said Mick earnestly, then blushed when everyone laughed. 'That's to say, it's for everybody – all ages. My Granny Colquohoun is coming down from Rothiemurchus, and – oh hell, you explain, Wendy.'

'Mick's mother wanted to have the party up at Balquhidder,' said Wendy, trying to keep a straight face, and not catch Winnie's eye. 'But Mick thought it would be more fun to have it here, partly because this really is the old family place, and partly because so many of Mick's friends are around here, at this time of year. So, the downstairs rooms of the Tower are to be poshed up for the reception and supper, and there's to be a big marquee on the square in front of the Tower for the dancing. All the family are coming – Mick's Mum and Dad, and his Granny, and my Mum and Dad. Some of the older folk are going to stay at the Covenanters Inn at Aberfoyle, but the young crowd are all bringing campbeds, and they're going to sleep in the Tower. It should be super fun, I think. We're inviting all the kids here at the moment who have come riding with us –'

'Patrons,' put in Mick, winking at Daisy.

'– so we should have a super mix of ages, and different sorts of people,' Wendy said. 'Do say you'll come, Mrs Graham.'

'I book you for the Eightsome Reel,' Angus told her.

'And I book you for the Lancers, so it's settled!' said Mick. 'Eight-thirty for nine. You'll get cards, of course. Winnie and Wendy are kindly addressing them – it keeps them out of mischief, you know.'

'I don't know why I put up with this,' said Winnie.

But something else had caught Daisy's attention.

'Mick,' she said, 'I want to ask you something. Are you going to sleep in the Tower?'

'I thought I might,' Mick told her. 'I haven't slept in there for years – not since I was in the Scouts. And it will be the last opportunity. Why do you ask?'

'I was wondering,' Daisy said, 'if you wouldn't be afraid of the ghost?'

'The ghost.' Mick looked at her with comic incredulity. 'What ghost?'

'The one who wails when the moon is out.'

'Oh, that one,' said Mick, teasingly. 'You've been talking to Mrs MacAlister, haven't you?' He raised his voice in a sing-song screech, and went on, 'You're an awful lad to scoff, Master Michael, but haven't I heard the poor lady crying and moaning all week with a broken heart, sic a to-do, and the moon full.'

Daisy could not help laughing, but she stood her ground.

'I have not been talking to Mrs MacAlister,' she said. 'Everyone knows there is a ghost, Mick.'

'Then everyone's cracked,' said Mick, making a face at her. 'There's no such thing as a ghost.'

'Yes, there is,' objected Wendy. 'Your father has heard her.'

'I suppose he was drunk at the time,' replied Mick, witheringly.

'Well, that's what his father says,' said Wendy to Daisy. 'Only some people are too sceptical for words.'

Bridget poured more coffee, and the conversation turned to the pleasures in store for them at the three-day camp.

It was now after eleven o'clock, and Daisy was exhausted. She had had more wine to drink than she had ever had before, and she felt funny in her head, as if her mind was joined to her body by a thread which might detach itself, and let her mind float away, at any moment. She did not listen to Angus's instructions about the camp, assuming that they would be repeated to her by someone else later; the talk buzzed about her, as meaningless as the humming of bees in a summer garden. As she sat on the sofa between Wendy and Angus, she looked at Mick Drummond sitting on the hearthrug. He alone seemed in focus, against a general background of fuzziness.

It was then that an extraordinary resemblance struck Daisy, one so unexpected that at first her mind would not let it in. But it would not go away. The fact was that Mick Drummond looked like Clementina. Of course it was ridiculous, and Daisy knew that, more than likely, she was drunk. How could that broad-nosed, wide-mouthed satyr's face be like the face of Clementina Rattray, straight-featured and beautiful, like a face stamped on a coin? Yet it was so. It was one of these likenesses that one sees sometimes among brothers and sisters; not a feature corresponds on cither face, yet the resemblance is so striking that you can't mistake it.

Daisy found herself wondering why she had never noticed before, and why no one else had ever mentioned it. But she could not think about it any more now. Her eyelids were getting heavier and heavier, Mick was receding into the blur that the room had become. Daisy's head dropped against Angus's shoulder, and she fell fast asleep.

11
Strife

Daisy had very little recollection next morning of how she had got to bed. In the vaguest way, she remembered stumbling upstairs, but could not think how she had got undressed and under her quilt. Now she felt terrible. She had a pain in her stomach, her mouth felt mouldy, and her eyeballs ached behind her smarting eyelids. It was agony, she discovered, to open her eyes, even before the curtains had been drawn back. She supposed that this was what is called a hangover, and knew that her mother would have been absolutely furious. Raising herself painfully on one elbow, Daisy squinted at the clock. Half-past eight. Across the room, Bridget was fast asleep with her mouth open. Clementina's bed was empty. She must have got up at her usual time, and gone out without making a sound. Daisy curled up again, clutching her stomach, and pulled the bedclothes over her head to shut out the light.

After a while, her mind cleared a little, and images of the night before began to float through it. Bridget in a blue dress, looking as good as gold. Speaking only when spoken to. Taking a back seat. Fishy. Angus, sitting by Clementina, never looking at her, rarely speaking to her, but all the time you were aware of the invisible bond between them, and you hoped that one day you would feel like that about someone too. Wendy and Winnie, red haired and cheerful, looking comically alike, although they were only cousins. Looking alike. That rang a bell, if your head would stand even the thought of bells ringing. Something else about looking alike. What could it have been? Then with a funny sensation in her chest, Daisy remembered. Mick Drummond and Clementina.

Daisy decided to get up then. However unpleasant, it was better than lying there in bed, fretting over all the queer and inexplicable problems which centred on Clementina Rattray. The most terrible thing was not being able to share her anxiety with anyone – not any one at all, she reflected dismally, as she went into the bathroom to wash, and splash cold water on her aching eyes. Even those she trusted most, her father and mother, would never understand; they would think that she had allowed her imagination to get the better of her in a bad and unhealthy way. In her mind's eye, Daisy could see their grave faces as they advised her to put such wicked nonsense out of her mind at once. But what nonsense? Even now Daisy could not put into words what it was she feared was happening. She only knew that if Clementina and Mick were indeed related, talk of coincidence would no longer do. All the strange things had happened because Clementina was connected to the Drummonds.

As she dressed, Daisy found herself clutching at a last straw. Perhaps she had been mistaken. Perhaps, late at night, when she had been half asleep, she had imagined a likeness which did not exist. She did not really believe this, but she thought she had better find out whether anyone else had noticed; for want of somebody better, she decided to ask Mrs Graham. So she combed her hair, avoided looking in the mirror, and went downstairs.

In the kitchen, Mrs Graham was sitting in the midst of the horrible debris of the previous night's meal. No tidying or washing-up had been done: dirty plates and glasses and cutlery were strewn everywhere, while on the table lay dishes with food remains withering unpleasantly around their rims. Mrs Graham was drinking black coffee and looking wrecked; she looked up at Daisy from the letter she was reading, raised an eyebrow, and pushed the coffee-pot towards her.

'All pleasures have to be paid for,' she remarked. 'Have some coffee.'

'No, thanks,' said Daisy.

'It's on prescription,' said Mrs Graham, pouring her a cup. 'It'll make you feel better. Will you help me wash up?'

'Yes, of course,' Daisy said.

She drank her coffee while Mrs Graham folded up her letter, put it away on a shelf behind the bread-bin, and set about tidying the kitchen. She scraped pots and dishes into the tidy bin, and stacked everything neatly on one side of the sink. While Daisy fetched clean drying-up cloths from a drawer, she filled the sink with hot, soapy water, and was ready to begin.

Mrs Graham washed, and Daisy dried, in silence. Daisy, remembering the amount of gin Mrs Graham had drunk, as well as wine, reckoned that she probably had a hangover worse than her own. This thought gave her a certain amount of self-righteous satisfaction, and she would have been disappointed to discover that it was not true. Mrs Graham never had hangovers; she was silent because she was thinking about a letter which had come in the morning post, and was laying plans in her mind.

Slowly the washing-up was reduced to orderly piles of clean dishes and clusters of shining glasses on the kitchen table. Daisy watched Mrs Graham draining the sink and wiping it round with a damp cloth. Then she said, 'Um – Harriet, I want to ask you something.'

'Sure,' said Mrs Graham.

'Well – last night,' went on Daisy, swallowing hard, 'last night it suddenly occurred to me that Mick Drummond is really very like Clementina to look at, and I just wondered – had you ever noticed it too?'

Mrs Graham turned from the sink to look at her, and before she opened her mouth Daisy knew she had been a fool to ask.

'Mick Drummond?' screeched Mrs Graham, incredulously. 'Like Clementina? I'd have thought they were as different as Beauty and the Beast. Oh, come on, kid. I know you'd had a lot more wine than you're used to, but – well, honestly!'

Daisy felt herself going scarlet with anger, but she just managed to prevent herself from retorting, 'And whose fault was it if I had a lot more wine than I'm used to?' Instead, she choked down her annoyance, shrugged her shoulders, and said tightly, 'Oh, well, never mind. It seemed so to me at the time.'

Perhaps Mrs Graham realised that she had offended her, for she tried, clumsily, to turn the whole thing into a joke.

'It's odd, though, isn't it, how you sometimes imagine likenesses in the most unlikely people?' she said, with a return to her usual burbling tone. 'Or sometimes animals. There are two portraits in the Art Gallery at home, of a Mr and Mrs Haddo of Muchalls – or is it Muchalls of Haddo? Anyway, I don't know if you've ever noticed, but he's like a pig in a frock coat, and she's like a poodle in corsets.'

Daisy let the joke misfire. She got busy sorting out the cutlery, and putting it away in a drawer. Mrs Graham hung up the dishcloths to dry, then she said, 'Daisy, do you want to hear my good news?'

'Yes,' Daisy replied, automatically.

She turned round, and saw Mrs Graham looking very pink and pleased with herself. For the first time ever,

Daisy found her unbearable. She was as self-absorbed as Bridget was.

'I've got a new job,' said Mrs Graham coyly. 'As Director of Social Services at Reading. Awfully high-powered. You can congratulate me, dear.'

'I do,' said Daisy stonily.

'So I'm afraid,' Mrs Graham went on, 'that you'll have to look for another chum next term. Biddy and I shall have to start packing up just as soon as we get back to Aberdeen next week. But perhaps you'll come and stay with us in Reading some time.'

'Perhaps,' echoed Daisy.

But she knew that she never would, and she knew, in a moment of great clarity, that the Grahams would never ask her. They would go off to their new life, and after next year's Christmas card, she would never hear from them again. It was a great relief.

Not long after, Bridget came down looking cross, and Clementina appeared, carrying four addressed envelopes which she had found behind the front door. Each contained an identical printed card, with a name hand-written at the top.

MICHAEL DRUMMOND

requests the pleasure of your company at a

BALL

to celebrate his Coming of Age
to be held in

BENALMOND TOWER

on Saturday 29th July

9 p.m. *Fancy Dress* R.S.V.P.

On Mrs Graham's card, the words 'Fancy Dress' had been struck out with a pen.

'I suppose they think my dress is fancy enough as it is,' she said, and, when no one contradicted her, 'Well, I suppose I'll have to go, since these nice boys are so keen to have me. And making fancy dresses will keep you all occupied when you come back from the three-day camp.'

There certainly was no time to think about fancy dress before the three-day camp. For the rest of Saturday, no one seemed to feel up to anything much, apart from lying about, reading magazines and watching television. So Sunday was a day of rush and scurry, washing blouses and underwear, ironing, and packing up all the things they were going to need. They had been told that, as well as their personal kit, they must bring a share of the provisions; fourteen pounds of potatoes, six tins of baked beans, and two large meat pies. Mrs Graham baked these on Sunday evening.

Bridget, ever since the row with her mother, had gone silent. Daisy found this more upsetting than having her talking all the time. Knowing Bridget, Daisy thought it likely that she was planning some act of revenge, not against her mother, but against Clementina – and possibly Daisy herself – who had laughed at her. Daisy wished that she had even the tiniest clue as to what Bridget had in mind. Six days to go still, and plenty of scope for mischief.

The only conversation she had with Bridget was on Sunday afternoon, when they were both upstairs, trying to stuff enough gear for a large suitcase into two tiny haversacks. Then Bridget said abruptly, 'Mother says she's told you about her new job. Don't you wish you were me, leaving mouldy old Aberdeen, and going to a decent school in a decent town?'

'No, I don't,' Daisy replied coldly. 'I don't happen to

think Aberdeen's mouldy, and Reading's a dump, actually. I've been there, the year I went to Oxford with Dad, so you can take it from me.'

It was, and was not, a lie. She and her father had passed through Reading station on their way from Oxford to London, and she could not remember a single thing about it.

'Jealous,' sneered Bridget, but Daisy knew better than to take the matter any further. So silence dropped down again between them.

When Daisy, Bridget and Clementina arrived at the stables, on Monday morning, carrying their box of provisions, they found Mick pinning up a map on the wall outside the little office. The route they were to take was neatly marked on it in red ink.

'We'll wander through the forest to Balmaha today,' he said, after he had wished them good morning, 'then tomorrow we'll strike up the side of Loch Lomond to Inversnaid, where we'll turn east to Stronaclachar. On Wednesday we'll have a ride round the other side of Loch Katrine, and be home in time for tea. If you want to see who you'll be sharing tents with, and which nags you're to have,' he added, 'the lists are pinned up in the office.'

With which he rumpled Daisy's hair, and strode off in the direction of the paddock.

The three girls went into the office, where Wendy was sitting behind the desk, with a list of names and a mug of coffee in front of her. Bridget handed over her mother's cheque, and Wendy ticked off their names on her list.

'The tent list's over there,' she said, pointing to the opposite wall. 'There are supposed to be seven more people coming, but I don't suppose they're up yet.'

Then something unexpected, and, to Daisy, very embarrassing, occurred.

While Bridget was waiting for the receipt for their money – everything at the Trekking Centre was done efficiently – Daisy and Clementina wandered over to the tent list. Daisy was not much interested. She assumed she would be sharing with Bridget, and she was. She was surprised, however, and not very pleased to see Clementina's name bracketed with theirs in a group of three; she had supposed that Clementina would be sharing with her other friends. Of course there was nothing she could do about it, and she was about to turn away, when she realised that Clementina was not pleased either. In a blaze of anger the older girl turned, and said imperiously to Wendy, 'Who made this up?'

Wendy regarded her with unfriendly grey eyes.

'I did,' she said. 'Why? What's wrong with it?'

'What's wrong with it?' snapped Clementina. 'Everything's wrong with it. I don't want to share with *them*.'

'How rude of you to say so in front of them,' replied Wendy coolly. 'But I'm afraid it can't be helped you know. The only other girls coming are two sisters whom we don't know, and of course I've put them together. And I'm sharing with Winnie. So you're the odd one out, aren't you, Clementina?'

Daisy felt her mouth dropping open with surprise, and she closed it deliberately. She could scarcely believe her ears. It would never, for one moment, have occurred to her that Angus's friends had not accepted Clementina as one of themselves. She had always talked as if she were a welcome and well-liked member of the group. Yet there was real dislike in Wendy's voice. Suddenly, Daisy felt ill. She looked from Clementina's flushed, discomfited face to Bridget's eager, delighted one, and, yet again, she wanted to run away. She walked out of the office, and sat on a bench until Winnie came to open the harness room, and kit them out with hats and boots.

Mick's camps were well organised. A Range Rover, driven by one of his grooms, went ahead of the riders to the camping-ground, carrying tents, bedding and supplies. All the campers had to carry were their haversacks, and a sandwich lunch to eat on the way. These were distributed by Wendy before they moved down to the paddock for the allocation of the ponies. Five boys and two girls, none of whom they had met before, had joined the group; they seemed anxious to be friendly, and Daisy was thankful to see Bridget chatting quite brightly to two of the boys. But out of the tail of her eye Daisy could not help watching Clementina, sitting astride Gib with a face like thunder. She was shocked to discover that Clementina had such a temper, but then, she reflected, she really knew nothing about Clementina at all.

It was just after nine when the cavalcade, with Angus and Clementina in front, and Mick and Wendy in the rear, descended from the paddock, through the bracken and into the wood. The cool, pearly grey of the early morning was dissolving gradually as the sun's rays penetrated the mist, giving promise of a lovely day. And as the mysterious forest smell rose into her nostrils, and she felt the warmth of Tam's sturdy body under hers, Daisy thought with something approaching anger how unfair it was that she could not enjoy this lovely place as she ought. Other people had spoiled it for her, for ever.

The day passed, as days will. Birds sang, streams chuckled, waterfalls splashed as they rode through sunshine and shade, breathing in the sharp smells of earth and tree. They stopped to eat their sandwiches by a waterfall; in the afternoon they came out of the wood on to a tract of moorland, from which they wound down through bracken to the farm behind Balmaha where they were to spend the night. The Range Rover had been and gone, and all the camping gear was piled just inside the gate of the field which they were to use.

'Now, listen, people,' said Mick, when they were all through, and the gate was shut behind them, 'I'm going to divide you into three squads. Squad One will erect the tents. Squad Two will make the supper. Squad Three will attend to the ponies. There's a loo in the stable-yard which you're allowed to use, and a wash-basin for anyone who's too grand to be dirty. When your chores are done, you're free till supper-time – we'll make it seven thirty tonight, which will give you time to go down to the loch side, if you want to, or into the village.'

He fished a piece of paper out of his pocket, and read out the squads. Daisy was relieved to find that she was not in the same one as either Bridget or Clementina. Bridget was in Mick's squad, which was to put up tents, and Clementina was in the squad which went off with Angus to unsaddle the ponies, and feed and water them at the farm.

Daisy, who was in Wendy's cooking squad, spent the next hour contentedly enough, peeling potatoes and helping to gather wood for a camp-fire. The actual cooking was done on a rather smart camping gaz stove, but Wendy said the boys liked a proper fire for the singsong later. By dint of sticking to the people in her own squad, Daisy managed to get through the evening, too, without speaking to either of her room-mates; only when supper was over, and the camp-fire burning low, did she face the fact that she must spend the night with them. In the summer darkness which always lingers on the edge of day, she went down to the farmyard washroom, coming back slowly to the orange tepee marked Number Five. Reluctantly she unzipped the door, and crawled in.

Bridget was already in bed, hunched up unsociably and reading a paperback by the light of an electric torch. Daisy squirmed into the middle sleeping-bag, leaving the one on her left for Clementina, who had not yet turned up. They each had a thin, foam-rubber mattress underneath the feather sleeping-bag, but Daisy found it unyielding after the cushioned comfort of the holiday chalet.

'Ow, isn't it hard?' she said to Bridget, doing her best to sound normal. 'Not what we're used to, is it?'

'I'd have thought you would be used to it, where you live,' replied Bridget. 'In any case, since you're not even paying, you're hardly in a position to complain.'

Poor Daisy had a sudden, almost overwhelming desire to grab Bridget's torch out of her hand, and crack her hard over the head with it. But one just does not do these things. Instead, she tried once more.

'Oh, come on, Bid,' she said. 'Why be mean to me? I haven't done anything so very awful to annoy you, have I?'

Bridget shone her torch abruptly into Daisy's face, snapped it off, and wriggled down into her sleeping-bag.

'You?' she said into the darkness. 'You don't annoy me. You're too insignificant. I'll give Clementina Rattray that – she's not insignificant. You are.'

At this point, Daisy had finally had enough. This time, she did not try to stifle what came into her mind, but said it.

'You really should lay off, you know, Bridget. You're becoming obsessed. You could go nuts, the way you're carrying on.'

As she spoke, she knew it was a rotten thing to say, but she was past caring.

When Bridget answered, her voice was high with fury.

'I'm not the one who's nuts,' she said. 'She is. And a liar, and worse. But I'll pay her out, just wait. Ruining my holiday, and grabbing the only decent boy in this God-forsaken place.'

There was complete silence, and Daisy knew that Bridget was cursing herself in the darkness for what she had given away.

Eventually Daisy said quietly, 'So it was Angus you wanted all the time. Not Mick – that was just to annoy other people. Now I see. All this hating – it's jealousy, nothing else.'

'Oh, shut up,' said Bridget through her teeth, and pulled the flap of her sleeping-bag right over her head.

12
Flight

Next day, after they had had breakfast, groomed the ponies and taken down the tents, they rode up the eastern side of Loch Lomond to Inversnaid. It was another lovely morning, although Angus, who had a radio, told them that a change was forecast. It should have been delightful to jog along between the ruffled blue water of the loch and the upward sweep of the mountains, over springy grass spattered with daisies and frail harebells. But Daisy saw nothing, nor cared; the burden of other people's hatred lay on her heart like a cold stone.

She had managed to push Tam into a place in the line where she was not obliged to speak to anyone, and she rode a long way alone, thinking less about the queer events connected with Clementina than about the terrible loathing which Bridget felt for her. Until last night, Daisy had found it impossible to understand. Even if Clementina was a liar, as Bridget believed, her lying had not damaged Bridget, and surely you could not detest anyone so heartily because she had laughed at you, or forgotten to bring you breakfast in bed. Now, perhaps, it was a little easier to understand. Bridget was nearly a year older than Daisy, and boy-friends were very important in her life. Daisy could see that it would have been a great triumph for Bridget had Angus Wishart wanted to be her holiday boy-friend. But to hate so much, so bitterly, over such a thing ... Daisy was ashamed of her remark to Bridget in the tent the night before, but she was beginning to wonder, seriously, whether her suggestion might be true.

Presently, Clementina came riding down the side of the line on Gib, and fell in beside Daisy, the path at this point being wide enough for two. Daisy did not welcome her, but could hardly tell her to go away, so they rode in silence for a while. Daisy's feelings about Clementina were now very confused. Apart from the feelings of strangeness and foreboding which the girl aroused in her, her former belief that Clementina was really a nice person had received a rude jolt the previous morning, when Clementina had been so nasty about the sleeping arrangements at the camp. And yet – Daisy knew now that unhappiness made people nasty who weren't nasty by nature. Hadn't she herself been hateful to Bridget last night in the tent? That Clementina was unhappy must be obvious to anyone who looked at her. But Daisy was too weary to make the effort to be friendly any more. She glanced sidelong at Clementina's pale face and wondered why she was there.

It took some time for Clementina to come to the point. At last, she said, 'I hope I didn't disturb you when I came into the tent last night.'

She had come in after midnight, and had disturbed Daisy by crawling all over her in the dark.

'Not at all,' said Daisy, with tired politeness.

'We all went down to the village, to the pub,' said Clementina. 'You know, Mick and Angus and the rest.'

'You're too young to go into pubs,' said Daisy reprovingly. 'It isn't fair. You could get the manager into trouble.'

'Oh, I look far older than I am,' said Clementina carelessly. 'What a stuffy kid you are, Daisy. Anyway, that's where I was, if you were wondering.'

Daisy knew exactly what she meant, and felt inclined to retort that she hadn't been wondering, because she could safely leave that kind of wondering to Bridget. Instead, she said flatly, 'You don't have to tell me what you do. It's no business of mine, and I couldn't care less. You can do what you like.'

Clementina said no more, but reined Gib in, and let Daisy ride on in front of her. Daisy sighed, and wished she had said something else. Tears came into her eyes, and she wanted most desperately to go home.

After lunch, which they ate by the lochside, they turned east into the forest again.

'We should make Stronaclachar by five,' said Mick, 'then it will be the same routine as last night – though I'm afraid it won't be so pleasant.' He pointed back down the loch to where woolly black bales of cloud were massing on the rim of a clear sky. 'However, it can't be helped,' he went on, 'and with luck we should get the tents up before the downpour.'

This proved over-optimistic. It was mid afternoon before the clouds moved at all, but then, pushed by a small, chill wind, they wiped out the blue sky in half an hour. There was much opening of haversacks and putting on of jerseys; Daisy put on her cagoule as well, as she supposed it was soon going to rain. But the wind seemed to keep the rain at bay for a while; they had passed the deserted pier at Stronaclachar, lapped by the black water of Loch Katrine, and ridden a mile to their campsite before the first spots fell. They dismounted in a field next to a cluster of stone and slate farm buildings; Mick's groom had already erected a large green tent in the middle of the field, and had left all their other gear piled alongside it.

'Right,' Mick said urgently. 'It's going to rain, and it isn't going to stop, so the sooner we get the tents up, and our chores done, the drier we shall be. The big tent's the common-room, and we'll eat there, when everyone is ready.'

There followed a ghastly evening.

Daisy and her fellow cooks were lucky, because they were sheltered by the tent while they worked, a privilege remarked on enviously by almost everyone else when they arrived, wet and windblown, from their tasks outside. Presently, the tent was full of people, sitting on rugs around the stove; the smell of wet hair and clothes mingled stuffily with the smell of cooking stew. Wendy was a bit on edge because, she said to Daisy, it wasn't ideal to have so many people in a confined space with a gas stove in the centre. Every time someone moved, she said snappily, 'Oh, do sit down, please. Do you want to cause an accident?' She said it to Bridget, who had been looking thunderous before. Afterwards, Daisy didn't dare to look at her.

When Clementina came in with Angus, she didn't look too pleased either. Only Mick and Winnie were persistently cheerful, although Wendy also recovered her good temper after the meal had been served and the stove lifted out under the awning.

Then Mick organised some games, and Angus, who played the guitar, made a half-hearted attempt to get another singsong under way. But

We're off to see the Wild West Show,
The elephant and the kangaroo-hoo-hoo,
Never mind the weather —

did not seem so amusing tonight, with a chill draught blowing through the tent-flap, and rain drumming on the canvas overhead. Before long, most people were saying good-night, pulling on their waterproofs, and making a dash for bed.

Daisy decided not to go down to the farm, but to go to the loo and clean her teeth behind a gorse bush. When she got to the tent, Bridget was already in bed, and she had scarcely had time to get undressed and into her sleeping-bag when Clementina arrived. She took off her shoes and socks, and began wriggling out of her trousers and into her sleeping-bag. In the gloom, Daisy watched Bridget watching Clementina, and hoped fervently that Bridget would leave well alone. But she knew it was too much to ask.

'Good heavens,' Bridget began, affecting great astonishment. 'Can it be that the lovely Miss Rattray is going to favour us with her company tonight? Has Mr Wishart seen sense, and turned her out, one wonders? Or does she plan to wait till we're asleep, and go sneaking off again?' Her tone changed abruptly, and she added coldly, 'You really needn't bother, you know, dear. It's fairly obvious what's going on.'

Clementina was silent for a moment, while she adjusted elaborately the pillow end of her sleeping-bag, and made herself comfortable. Then she said in her cool, superior voice, 'You have a mean little mind, Bridget Graham. I don't know how a nice woman like your mother managed to produce you. But for your information – as I told your prim little chum this morning – I haven't been sleeping with Angus. I do have principles, and I wouldn't, while I'm your mother's guest. And anyway —' the cool voice suddenly became triumphant '— there will be plenty of time later. Angus and I are engaged, you see. When I go to London, he's coming too, and we're going to get a flat, and live together until we can afford to get married. We're going to have the most marvellous life together. Don't you wish you were me, Bridget? Wouldn't you like to be engaged to Angus yourself? Go on, admit it. You'd like it better than anything, wouldn't you, my dear?'

At this moment, something inside Daisy seemed to snap. Before Bridget had time to reply, she knew that she could not spend the night in the same place as these two enemies. She had to get out. Hardly knowing what she was doing, she battled her way out of her sleeping-bag, pulled on a jersey, and unzipped the tent door with trembling fingers. Then she ran out into the rain in her bare feet, over the soaking grass, and down through bracken into a scrubby little wood. She might have run through it, and into the dark waters of the loch, had she not caught her foot on a bramble sucker, and fallen flat on her face among the ferns. She lay there in the wet, sobbing soundlessly, until a pair of strong arms lifted her, and turned her over, and picked her up as if she were no weightier than a kitten. In the gathering darkness, Daisy looked up into the kind, swarthy face of Mick Drummond.

13

Mick's Story

'Now then, Shorty,' said Mick. 'This won't do. I can't have people dying of exposure on one of my camps. It would be bad for business, you know.'

Daisy was astounded by this sudden turn of events, and because she did not know what to say, lay still in his arms while he carried her back to the field. Mick strode over the grass to his own tent, which was dimly lit by a small electric lamp suspended from the ridge on a hook. Here he set her down on his camp-bed, and gave her a towel and a warm tartan rug.

'Dry your feet and take off your jersey,' he commanded. 'Then wrap yourself up in the rug. Don't move till I get back.'

He went out, dropping the tent-flap behind him. Daisy just had time to obey his instructions when he was back, carrying a thermos jug and two tin mugs. Sitting down on the bed beside her, he poured hot, steaming coffee into the mugs, and put one into her hands.

'There now,' he said. 'Are you warm enough? And dry?'

Daisy nodded speechlessly, and took a welcome sip of the coffee.

'Good,' said Mick. 'Then it's time for you and me to have a little talk. OK?'

Daisy found her voice.

'Yes,' she said. 'If you tell me what you want to know.'

Mick took a swig of his coffee, and looked at her thoughtfully in the faint light.

'It really depends,' he said, 'on what you're prepared to tell me. I can't make you tell me anything, although I suspect you very much need to talk to somebody. I've been worried about you for ages. No kid of your age should look so scared and miserable on holiday, and in the most beautiful country God ever made. Anyway – why don't you begin by explaining why I should have been coming back from the farm twenty minutes ago, to see you whipping across the field in your bare feet, as if all the hounds of hell were after you.'

Daisy hesitated, then suddenly realised that she could tell him anything.

'I just couldn't stand it any more,' she explained. 'I've been cooped up for nearly a month with two people who can't stand the sight of each other, and tonight, in the tent, they were having the most awful quarrel – Bridget and Clementina, you know.'

'Clementina,' repeated Mick grimly. 'I might have known she'd be mixed up in it somewhere. Born to make trouble, that girl was.'

If Daisy had not witnessed the little scene between Wendy and Clementina the previous morning, this speech would have taken her completely by surprise. Even as it was, she was shocked by the bitterness in Mick's voice. She shook her head helplessly.

'I – I thought you liked her,' she said. 'You all seemed to be such good friends. She was so keen to have you all to supper, and so pleased that you had offered to take Gib up to Balquhidder, so that she could ride him when she came to stay with you.'

'Pleased that I had *what*?' spluttered Mick incredulously. 'It's the first I've heard of it, believe me. It must have been Angus's idea – like getting her to invite us to supper. We only agreed for his sake. Poor chap, I think he thought it would improve her image in my eyes. He's bewitched, you see. None of the rest of us like her – but if he does, we have to accept her, or lose him.' He sighed, and went on sadly, 'Although I'm afraid we're going to lose him anyway. It was all fixed for him to go to the West of Scotland Agricultural College in the autumn, so that he could learn to factor our estate, but now he says he won't go. He spends half the day ringing up colleges round London, trying to get a place – but of course it's hopeless, so late in the year.'

Mick's voice had become harsh with disappointment, and Daisy realised how much he would mind if this long-cherished plan for Angus's future came to nothing.

'He wants to be your factor, Mick,' she said gently. 'He told Mrs Graham one evening that he has never wanted anything else in his life.'

Mick gave her a grateful look, but he went on, 'I'm sure he never has. But he wants something else now, and I don't think he can have both.'

Daisy drank some more of her coffee, and thought for a moment or two. Then she said, 'Is that the only reason why you don't like her, Mick? Because she might take Angus away?'

'No,' said Mick. 'It's not just that. She's not straightforward – she's fishy, somehow. I mean – well, it's obvious that she's related to my family in some way, and will she admit it? Oh, no. Now, what I want to know is, why shouldn't she admit it? Even if she doesn't believe in titles, and that sort of thing, it's hardly something to be ashamed of.'

Daisy heard the hurt pride in his voice, but all she said was, 'The night you came to supper – I thought she looked like you. But when I mentioned it to Mrs Graham, she said I was daft.'

'That was very perceptive of you,' said Mick thoughtfully. 'Actually, it's not me she looks like as much as some of the women in my family. We have portraits in my parents' house at Balquhidder that could be her in eighteenth century clothes. And of course, Clementina Rattray is a family name. But when I mentioned it to her, she got in the most awful tizzy, saying she'd never heard of the Drummonds, and who were they, anyway? Positively offensive, she was. And then she clammed up, and has hardly spoken to me since, which is damned awkward, since every time I turn round, there she is, staring at me.' He paused, then went on stubbornly, 'Anyway, she can say what she likes. Whoever she is, she's related to the Drummonds. Her face has been over our drawing-room fireplace all my life. I noticed the resemblance the first day I ever saw her, the day she made friends with that ill-natured creature, Billy. And that's another thing. Why does she have to pretend she's never ridden before? Does she think we were all born yesterday? No one could handle that animal the way she does who hadn't been born in the saddle.'

Mick stopped, out of breath. It occurred to Daisy that, so far, he had told her a great deal more than she had told him. Perhaps he guessed what she was thinking, for he caught her eye, and grinned.

'Sorry,' he said.

Daisy finished her coffee, and put the mug down on the groundsheet. She wrapped the rug around her bare toes, and said slowly, 'I think – it isn't as straightforward as it seems, Mick. Bridget would agree with you – she thinks Clementina is just a liar, and a cheat. But I don't. I don't think she ever had ridden before she came here, and I think she's too frightened to admit she might be related to your family. You see – a lot of terribly odd things have happened since we came here – uncanny, really – all involving Clementina. I've come to the conclusion that she isn't as nice a girl as I once thought she was, but to be fair – I also think she's scared half to death.'

She was afraid to look up at him. If she did, and saw disbelief in his eyes, she was on her own again. But when she made herself look, he was watching her with intense interest, and nothing else.

'Are you going to tell me what you mean by all this?' he asked.

'Yes,' said Daisy. 'I think you will believe me, and it will be a relief to tell you.'

And she did tell him. She could not have believed how easy it would be to let it all come tumbling out, about the odd way Clementina had behaved, that first day when she saw Benalmond Tower, how she had called Angus by his name, how she had known, without being told, about the Redcoats coming to Benalmond, and being blamed for setting fire to the stables. She told him about the strange remark Clementina had made in her sleep, 'It wasn't the Redcoats, Angus. They didn't go back to the stables. It was Charlie. I know it was Charlie.' She told him about Clementina's extraordinary reaction to their finding the little tower room, about the Jacobite airs Clementina had played on her violin, and finally – not without a pang of disloyalty – about the grant application form for St Cecilia's College of Music. When, at last, her voice ran out into silence, she and Mick sat in the light of the little lamp, watching each other as the wind sucked around the tent walls, and the rain tap-danced on the canvas roof.

Daisy could not read his expression; she thought she saw puzzlement, and shock, and pain – and – could it be fear?

To break the silence, she said, 'You do believe me, don't you, Mick?'

'Oh, yes,' Mick said. 'I believe you. You see – it all ties up. But it's rum, Daisy. By God, it's rum.'

'What do you mean, it all ties up?' Daisy wanted to know.

She crept closer to him along the camp-bed; he put a hard young arm round her, and held her close to his side. They sat like that for some time, then Mick said reluctantly, 'It ties up – with something that happened long ago. Something that she couldn't know about – in any natural way.'

'What happened long ago?' Daisy asked.

Mick seemed to hesitate, then he said, 'Well – I'll tell you. I think you ought to know – something of what happened, anyway. It was away back in the eighteenth century. In 1726, I think it was, one of my ancestors, Gavin Drummond, married Arabella Rattray of Glener-och, a very rich, headstrong lady. When she came to Benalmond as a bride, she brought with her a little girl of two years old, called Clementina Borde. Arabella said this child was the illegitimate daughter of her former companion and lady's maid, Elizabeth Borde, who had died of smallpox just after the baby was born. Unfortunately, family resemblance soon proved this story untrue – the child was the image of Arabella, and it was pretty obvious to everyone whose daughter the little Clementina really was. However, people were scared of Arabella, and I don't suppose her story was ever challenged – openly, at least. The next year, Arabella gave birth to another daughter – legitimately, this time – who was baptised Charlotte Arabella.'

'Charlie,' said Daisy.

'Yes, Charlie. There were other children, all boys – the eldest, Michael, succeeded to the estates when his father had to flee to France after the unfortunate affair of 1745.'

'He was a Jacobite,' said Daisy.

'Yes. But never mind him. The story I'm telling you is about Charlotte and Clementina. Remember that they were half-sisters, though one was Miss Drummond of

Benalmond, and the other supposed to be the daughter of a penniless lady's-maid. These two girls grew up in the same house, but in very different situations, and it's not surprising if they detested each other pretty heartily. It must have been obvious to Charlotte who Clementina was, and she lost no opportunity to hurt and humiliate her. Lady Arabella had the idea of educating the two girls together – perhaps she had a bad conscience – and, unfortunately for their relationship, Clementina was everything that Charlotte was not – handsome, clever, musical, and a splendid horsewoman. And then, to crown all, they had to fall in love with the same man.'

'What was his name?' asked Daisy, fascinated.

Mick hesitated, then said hurriedly, 'I don't remember.' For the first time, Daisy sensed that he was not telling her the truth. But before she could say any more he went on quickly, 'He was only a stableman – someone who normally wouldn't even have been noticed by hoity-toity Miss Charlotte Drummond. But it seems that anything Clementina had, she wanted too. It didn't help harmony much when the stableman made it clear that he preferred Clementina Borde.'

'What happened?' Daisy asked. 'Did he marry her?'

'No. He was killed in an accident. Charlotte married a skinny young laird from up Glen Prosen – she was a plain, sandy lass, but she had a fine dowry which probably made up for her lack of looks. I don't know whether Clementina ever married – she may have done. I've just never heard.'

'The ghost,' Daisy whispered, her brown eyes widening in the shadowy tent. 'She became a ghost, Mick.'

'There's no such thing as a ghost,' said Mick impatiently. 'People hear a story, and they invent a ghost to go with it. And don't tell me my father's heard it, because he hasn't. He's the world's greatest tall story teller, and I bet he told Wendy this one just to hear her squeal. But this other business – God, it's queer, Daisy. It's the queerest thing I've ever heard. I wonder if Angus knows.'

'I don't think so,' Daisy said. 'I don't think Clementina has told anyone. I don't think she can.'

Mick unscrewed the top from his thermos, and poured them each another half mug of coffee.

'Here, drink this,' he said. 'Then I'm going to fetch a spare bedding roll, and take you over to Wen and Win for the rest of the night. I don't suppose we'll ever understand this affair completely, it's too bizarre – but some things do become clearer – like why she's so keen to get him away to London with her. You couldn't imagine her settling down very happily as factor's wife at Balquhidder after this, could you? I don't fancy it much myself, to tell you the truth.'

'Maybe I shouldn't have told you,' said Daisy unhappily.

'I'd have thought very little of you if you hadn't,' said Mick, as he put on his oilskin, and felt about in the shadows for his boots.

14
A Morning Walk

Daisy had supposed, as Mick carried her over the grass to Wendy's tent, that she would not sleep a wink. Instead, she slept deeply and dreamlessly, and when she woke it was to find herself alone under warm, sunlit canvas, with the delicious smell of grass-in-a-tent tickling her nose. Wendy and Winnie had rolled up their bedding and departed, leaving a note pinned to Daisy's sleeping-bag. It said, 'STAY PUT TILL I COME BACK. YOU HAVE NO TROUSERS!!! WIN.'

So Daisy lay still in her cosy nest, and thought about her strange encounter with Mick the night before. He had been so kind, and it had been a great relief to tell – and be believed by – someone older and more responsible than she was. And yet – she turned over uneasily and bit her finger-nail – she knew that nothing had really been explained. It wasn't enough to say, isn't it queer? Isn't it rum? Surely the next thing you had to ask was, why has this happened, and what is likely to happen as a result? Daisy wondered too why Mick had been so evasive about the end of his story. She was convinced that he knew more than he was willing to tell. She made up her mind that if she could corner him today, just for a few minutes, she would ask him ... but as things turned out, she did not have to do so.

When Winnie arrived, she was laden with a mug of coffee, a bacon roll, Daisy's haversack, her boots, and her denim jeans.

'Morning, lazybones,' she said cheerfully. 'Mr Drummond's compliments, and if you've nothing else planned, he'd like you to walk over to the Forestry Lodge with him to fetch some eggs. There's no need to rush – we have plenty of time. We haven't far to go today, so we're going to have an early lunch here before we push off.'

She laid down her burdens, and was out of the tent before Daisy had time to thank her properly. So Daisy ate her roll, and drank her coffee, and wondered why on earth these people were being so nice to her. When she had finished, she got up, dressed, and nipped down to the farmyard with her sponge-bag. It was a sharply bright, rain-washed morning, and smelt renewed. The cobbles in the yard were drying in patches which grew larger as you watched them. Angus and his squad were feeding the ponies; Angus gave her a wave, but Clementina ignored her completely.

'Gosh, it's going to be one big, happy family when we get back to the chalet,' thought Daisy, and surprised herself by giggling into her face flannel. When she returned to the field, Mick was sitting on the gate, wearing jeans and the tattiest old jersey Daisy had ever seen.

'Good morning,' he greeted her. 'I hear you slept very well indeed. So did I. Odd, isn't it? And now —' he jumped down from the gate and rubbed his hands on the seat of his pants '— would you care for a walk? It isn't far, and we need eggs to scramble for lunch.'

'I'd like to,' said Daisy, and after she had put her sponge-bag back in her haversack, they set off, beating a way through the soaking bracken as they went upland. Soon they were on a footpath which ran through heather which was within days of bursting into its fiery August flower.

It was about a mile to the Forestry Lodge, a squat

pine-and-shingle building in the middle of a plantation. The forester's wife kept hens. For most of the way the track was wide enough for two, and they walked in companionable silence for a while. When Mick did eventually speak, it was to discuss something quite unconnected with the thing which was uppermost in Daisy's mind.

'Daisy,' he said, 'I want to ask you something. Wendy and I were planning to get married as soon as I was twenty-one, as you probably know. But she's just newly eighteen, and her parents have decided that they want her to go to University first. So – amid groans – we've agreed to wait. The point is – she'll be going to Aberdeen in October to study Maths, and as she doesn't know a soul north of Balquhidder, I rather wondered if you and your family might befriend her, and ask her to supper once in a while, you know. Wendy's really shy with strangers, and she's never been away on her own before, not even to school. Do you think your mother would mind?'

'No. She'd be delighted,' said Daisy, both astonished and pleased. 'But would Wendy really like to come? It's terribly noisy, and full of babies and things.'

'She'd love it. She asked me to ask you, actually.'

'Did she? Then I'll give her our telephone number.' Daisy paused for a moment, then she added shyly, 'I suppose you'll be coming to Aberdeen to see her, some week-ends?'

'I surely will,' agreed Mick.

'Because if ever you need a bed, you can stay with us, you know.'

'Can I? What a nice idea. Wouldn't it be a nuisance?'

'No,' Daisy assured him. 'Our house goes like a fair. There are always people staying, or having supper, or something.'

As she said it, she realised that it sounded more like a

Graham remark than a Bradbrook one. But it was true, all the same. Perhaps her parents just took hospitality for granted, and so she did, too.

'Then if you're sure you can fit me in, I'd love to come,' Mick told her. 'Remember to give me your phone number too, and tell your mother I'll be coming.'

Daisy walked on in a cloud of delight. Not until they had been to the Lodge, and were retracing their steps with the eggs in plastic containers, did she remember that there were things she wanted to ask Mick. It was as if a chill little wind came out of nowhere, and blew her pleasure in the future away. She still had to cope with the perils of here and now.

'Mick,' she said hesitantly, 'may I ask you something?'

'Of course,' he said. 'I've been expecting it.'

They had come to a stile. He seated himself on the top of it, she on the step lower down.

'It's what we were talking about last night,' Daisy said.

'I'm sure it is. Come on – out with it then.'

'Well,' said Daisy, 'I've been thinking. There has to be an explanation – a reason why Clementina knows all the things about your family that you told me last night really happened. What do you think the reason is, Mick?'

Mick did not answer at once. He sat looking down at her from his perch, his eyes thoughtful beneath his slightly frowning brow. Then he said unwillingly, 'It sounds so far-fetched when you put it into words. But I suppose I think she must have lived before – as Clementina Borde – and that coming here to Benalmond has in some way jogged her memory, so that she's remembering what happened to her then. A lot of people do believe that sort of thing. Until now I haven't been one of them.'

Daisy nodded seriously.

'Yes. I've wondered that, too,' she said. 'I'd like to believe it, actually, because although it would be queer, it wouldn't be dangerous, would it? Just remembering?'

Mick stared at her.

'Dangerous?' he repeated. 'No – I don't suppose it would be dangerous. What are you getting at, Daisy?'

Daisy took a moment to assemble her thoughts.

'Look,' she said. 'There's another possibility, isn't there? Let's suppose that she never was Clementina Borde, but is just an ordinary person, living a once-only life. Still, there are – similarities. You said last night that the Clementina in the story was very clever, and musical, and a wonderful horsewoman. So is Clementina now. And Clementina now not only knows about the past – she's scared by it – scared half to death by the mention of the name 'Charlie'. What I wonder is this. Do you suppose that history could be repeating itself? This holiday we're on is called a time-sharing holiday. Do you suppose that Clementina may have become involved in a different kind of time-sharing? And that she knows what she does because what happened long ago is happening again? That could be very dangerous – depending on the end of the story.'

'No!' cried Mick, with a violent, sobbing sound. He leaped down from the stile, and beat upon it with his fists so furiously that Daisy looked up at him in terror. She saw that his face had gone as white as paper, and he was trembling all over. He must have seen her alarm, because he made a great effort to control his agitation. 'No,' he repeated, more quietly, then, eagerly, as if to convince himself more than her. 'It's impossible. The circumstances are not the same. It couldn't happen again.'

'If you told me what did happen —'

Mick shook his head. Suddenly, the tone of his voice changed, and Daisy saw him struggling to assume a carefree attitude, and his words came tumbling out, far too plausibly. 'No, no, Shorty. It's too silly. I'm not going to tell you because it would worry you, especially if you are going to start thinking along lines of history repeating itself. How could it possibly? I mean – the facts are totally different. There's no jealous daughter of the house now, is there? Only me, and a little brother called James.'

Then the words, 'There's Bridget,' formed themselves in Daisy's mind, but she dared not speak them aloud.

Mick helped her over the stile, and they went down through the sea of fern to the camp.

15
Waiting

They got back to the chalet just after six, Bridget, Clementina and Daisy, and went upstairs to bath and change. Apart from the icily polite, 'Would you like to go first?' and, 'No, after you,' type of exchange, not a word was said, and it was by chance that they were all ready to come downstairs at the same time. Mrs Graham was in the kitchen, writing letters at the table. She greeted them without enthusiasm.

'Oh, dear, you're back, are you? Not hungry, I hope? I can tell from your happy little faces that you've had an absolutely marvellous time.'

'Simply lovely,' said Bridget snappishly.

'We've all fallen out,' Clementina announced in her clear, cold voice. 'As you know, I'm devoted to you, Harriet, but I just can't take to your daughter, and as for her little good-as-gold friend, you can't imagine what a snake-in-the-grass she has turned out to be. So I hope you won't mind if I don't speak to either of them between now and Sunday.'

Mrs Graham was much amused by this ungracious speech.

'Not at all, my dear,' she said. 'Feel free to ignore them completely – although I must say I thought that was what you had been doing ever since you arrived. Now what have you been up to, Daisy, to incur such disfavour? I've always found you quite inoffensive.'

'She's been poaching,' put in Bridget sharply. 'Sucking

up to Clementina's posh friends. Only Clementina is allowed to do that.'

Daisy went very pink in the face.

'I have not been sucking up to them,' she said, with dignity. 'They have been sucking up to me. I hope the difference is clear to everyone.'

The absurdity of this speech struck her even before she had got to the end of it. She caught Mrs Graham's eye, and laughed. Really, it was impossible not to like Mrs Graham. Even when you knew she was completely self-centred and that her easy-going attitude covered an unwillingness ever to take a stand about anything, you couldn't help finding her nice and amusing. Her kindness was real enough, even if it didn't go very deep.

It was obvious that she was not in the least interested in what had happened at the camp, because she immediately turned the conversation to her own affairs.

'You'll be pleased to know, Biddy, that I've managed to sell our annual four weeks in this shack to Jerry Briggs – at a small profit. He thinks it will be nice for his grandchildren. But I'm warning you now – no more dotty schemes. I'm going to Australia to see my sisters next summer. You may come, or not. Please yourself.'

'I'll come. I wish we had gone this year,' said Bridget peevishly.

Daisy wished most fervently that they had.

After supper that evening, Daisy went down on to the shore, and sat on the sandy bank under the birch trees. The stress of the last twenty-four hours had been overwhelming, and she wanted to be on her own for a little, to think.

It was a tremendous relief to her that Mick had believed her story – had he not done so, she thought she really would have run away. And, of course, the story he had told her about the two jealous girls had made clear the connection between Clementina and the past – up to a point. But – Daisy thought, as she watched with uncaring eyes the gentle little waves purring up the shingle – there was still a great deal which was not clear, and Mick was not going to make it so. For reasons of his own, he had no intention of telling her the end of his story, and that was alarming. For, Daisy wondered, if he really believed his own theory – that Clementina had once been Clementina Borde, and was now only remembering what had happened long ago – why should he be so reluctant to tell what else she might have remembered? Remembering might be uncomfortable, but it couldn't be dangerous. If, on the other hand, Mick secretly believed Daisy's theory – that past events were occurring, because time-sharing could have another meaning besides the obvious one – was he afraid of telling what had happened, for fear of making it come true? Daisy was sure that this was what he did believe, and that the end of the old story had been tragic; why else should he have been so distressed that morning, at the stile?

Daisy shivered, not entirely because of the chill evening air.

She thought for a while about reincarnation. Could one live again, and remember one's past experience, in a former life? Some people did believe that one could, although she knew how disapproving her father would have been of such a notion. In Clementina's case, though, there was one great obstacle to the solution that she was merely recalling the past of another person.

Daisy got up from the bank, because she was becoming very cold, and, buttoning up her cardigan, began to pace along the shore.

The obstacle was the horse – Billy, or Gib, or whatever you liked to call him. No doubt, Daisy thought, if one knew the details, one would discover that Clementina

Borde had a horse called Gib, whom no one else could ride. The point was that the present-day Clementina was not remembering someone else's experience – she had become, overnight, it seemed, an expert horsewoman in her own right. She had befriended, and controlled, a twentieth century, flesh-and-blood horse with a bad reputation. Unless you believed that the eighteenth century Gib had been born again as Billy ... Daisy decided that, even in this situation, where belief was being stretched to its limits, that was going too far.

So – assuming that her theory was the right one – what then? The question surely was this. Must the whole story, whatever it was, be re-enacted, with Bridget in the role of Charlotte Drummond, or could anything be done to stop it? For Daisy had no doubt that this was the part Bridget was to play. It did not matter that she was not Clementina's half-sister now; she was the jealous daughter of the house, in love with Clementina's man ... Daisy reached the landing-stage, and turned back towards the chalet with a coldness about her heart. If she did not know the end of the story, she could do nothing to stop its happening again – and if the end were not a tragic one, why should this awful scent of impending disaster hang upon the air?

There was nothing for it now but to wait, and count the hours, and hope against hope for escape. Daisy was thankful to see that Clementina and Bridget were keeping out of each other's way; she kept out of theirs, and watched them from a distance. Clementina spent nearly all her time at the stables; if Mick and Wendy did not want her there, either she did not know, or did not care. Bridget was busy in the sitting-room with yards of taffeta and a borrowed sewing-machine, making herself an eighteenth century costume for Mick's Fancy Dress Ball. She was a clever designer and dressmaker, and

Daisy knew that the finished dress would be beautiful. She herself had decided to go as a snowdrop; she had a pale green silk frock, and she made herself a petal hat out of white crêpe paper which Mrs Graham had bought for her on one of her trips to Glasgow. She was not in the mood to attempt anything more elaborate, and she told herself gloomily that she would feel a fool whatever she wore. Fortunately, the weather was fine, and, once the hat was made, she spent a lot of time out on the verandah, reading. When she was tired of books, she went for walks by herself, and usually, on the way back, she passed the front of Benalmond Tower.

Here all was now bustle and busyness; the doors, freshly painted, stood wide open, and women came and went with mops and pails. Windows downstairs were cleaned and opened, the steps banked with tubs of flowers and tiny trees. On Friday afternoon, a vast marquee was erected on the space in front of the door. A van loaded with electrical equipment drove up; workmen in overalls began to set up floodlighting, and coloured light bulbs were strung among the trees.

Daisy did not see Mick, not even in the distance, but he had told her not to expect to, when he had said goodbye after the camp. Tucking the piece of paper with her telephone number into his jerkin pocket, he had said, 'I'm going to be terribly busy for the next few days, but I'll see you at the Ball. Remember to keep a dance for me. And try not to worry. I'm sure it's only a case of someone psychic remembering things that happened long ago. Nothing can go wrong now. The situation is entirely different.'

Daisy disagreed, but she knew there was no point in arguing; she waited, and watched Bridget with an apprehensive eye.

Bridget, however, seemed absorbed in her dressmaking. Though she spoke very little to Daisy, and not at all to Clementina, she gave no sign that she was plotting mischief. Daisy swung between dread of some last minute calamity, and the desperate hope that after all Mick was right, and nothing could go wrong.

Saturday morning came, and, at last, Daisy could say, 'Tomorrow I'm going home.' She said it so often that the upsurge in her spirits turned her mood to one of optimism, which carried her through a morning of packing and an afternoon of walking around the estate. Of course, she told herself, Mick had been right. This time tomorrow, Clementina would be back at Torley Hall, and Bridget would be home in Aberdeen. What could possibly go wrong now? She came back, took her turn of the bathroom with the others, and put on her snowdrop costume.

'What on earth are you supposed to be?' demanded Bridget, who was certainly looking lovely in her gown of blue and green checked taffeta, with green ribbons woven into her hair.

'A daffodil,' said Daisy.

'Oh. You look more like a snowdrop,' Bridget said.

Daisy wondered how she had stood her for so long.

As usual, on such occasions, they were all ready far too soon. Mrs Graham, handsome if vast in red velvet, Daisy and Bridget were all down in the sitting-room by ten to eight, with their skirts spread out carefully beneath them so that they would not crease. Mrs Graham had said firmly at lunch-time that there was no need to leave before five to nine. They looked at one another without enthusiasm, and wondered how to pass the time. Mrs Graham went out to the kitchen to fetch herself a gin and tonic, and while she was there, Clementina came downstairs. She was bathed and made up, but wearing jeans and a jersey.

'I'm changing up at the Tower, with the others,' she said abruptly, to no one in particular.

'Oh, I thought you had changed,' Bridget could not resist remarking, foolishly.

Clementina had turned away, but now she turned back. She did not say anything, but she leaned against the doorpost giving Bridget a long, supercilious stare. Then she laughed, and departed.

Daisy hardly dared to look at Bridget, so sure she was that Bridget would be scarlet with rage. If there was one thing Bridget could not stand, it was to be laughed at. But when she did look, she saw that – more worryingly – Bridget was smiling.

'Just let her wait,' said Bridget. 'In a few hours, she won't be feeling so pleased with herself, I can tell you.'

'Whatever do you mean?' cried Daisy, in a fright.

'You'll see,' said Bridget, with an absurd air of mystery.

In an instant, panic engulfed Daisy. The certainty that the quarrel between Bridget and Clementina would end in disaster came flooding back to her.

'Oh, Bid,' she cried, 'please – don't do anything you'll be sorry for later. Don't hurt her – please!'

Bridget looked at her as if she had taken leave of her senses.

'Hurt her?' she repeated. 'I'm not going to hurt her. I'm going to expose her. Before tomorrow, I'm going to make sure that Mother and everyone else will know what a hypocrite she really is.'

'But how?'

'You'll see,' said Bridget, again with the mysterious air which a less overwrought Daisy would have found quite ridiculous.

For this silly speech of Bridget's ought to have relieved her. What did it mean, after all, except that Bridget was planning to make some sort of scene, which might be embarrassing, but could hardly be dangerous? But Daisy was in no state to reason this out now.

Terrible thoughts were teeming in her mind, but through them one came sharp and clear. She must find someone who could tell her the end of the story of the other Clementina; only if she knew that could she protect the Clementina she knew until morning. She knew that she could not run to Mick, and beg him to tell; this was his twenty-first birthday, and he was now with his family, getting ready for the Ball. For a moment, Daisy's mind went blank, then into its blankness came a voice. It belonged to Jerry Briggs, and she knew that an unspoken prayer had been answered.

'I heard the story from Mrs MacAlister, who runs the cafeteria, and is an expert on the Drummonds, self-styled.'

Then there was Mick's voice, laughing at her about the ghost.

'You've been talking to Mrs MacAlister, haven't you. . . .'

She had denied it, of course, but she knew she had to talk to Mrs MacAlister now. Without waiting to answer Mrs Graham's startled, 'Good heavens, child, what's the matter?' she ran out of the house in her fancy dress, banging the door shut behind her.

16
Mrs MacAlister

The cafeteria was housed in the long, low building which also held the games hall and the swimming-pool. When Daisy came panting up the steps that led to the terrace, with its row of umbrella shaded tables, a thin young man was locking the door, and putting up a shutter.

'Please,' Daisy gasped, holding her side, which had a stitch in it. 'Mrs MacAlister. I need to see Mrs MacAlister. Is she still here?'

The young man looked at her in gap-toothed amusement.

'Aye, she is, my wee fairy,' he said. 'Away round the back, and knock at the kitchen door. She'll be feeding her cat before she goes down to see all the fine folk arriving for Master Michael's Ball.'

So Daisy stumbled round the side of the building, skirted the dustbins, and hammered wildly on the back door. When Mrs MacAlister opened it, she cried out, 'Oh, Mrs MacAlister, I need you to tell me something, and if you can't tell me, I don't know what I'm going to do.'

Daisy had never seen Mrs MacAlister before in her life, and she would never see her again; afterwards it was not her round, apple-cheeked face she remembered as much as her bewilderment.

'Well now,' she said, putting down the saucer of milk she was holding, and drawing Daisy into the white-tiled empty kitchen, 'whoever you are, my wee flower, you had better come in, and tell me what it is I can tell you. Mercy on us, bairn, you're shaking like a leaf, and you all dressed up for the party, I see. Sit down. Would you like a cup of tea?'

Daisy shook her head. 'No, I haven't time,' she said. 'Thank you. Mrs MacAlister, you know all about the history of Benalmond, don't you?'

This was not, certainly, the question which Mrs MacAlister had expected, but here was a matter upon which she prided herself, and her face could not help assuming a modest, pleased expression.

'Och, not to say "all",' she said, sitting down opposite Daisy at a scrubbed table. 'Get away, Pussy, and catch a mouse. But I have an interest. The MacAlisters have been foresters to the Drummonds since the sixteenth century, you see.'

If she expected Daisy to be impressed by this, she was disappointed. A thick mist was obscuring everything in Daisy's mind except the questions she wanted to ask. She was not interested in the lineage of the MacAlisters. Mrs MacAlister watched her for a moment in perplexity, then she went on, 'What is it you want, dearie?'

With great effort, Daisy organised her words.

'Well – in the eighteenth century – there were two girls, called Charlotte Drummond and Clementina Borde.' Mrs MacAlister nodded. 'I know they didn't get on well, and I know they were both in love with the same man – a stableman, I believe he was. I know that Charlotte married a laird from up Glen Prosen, and I know that the stableman was killed in an accident.'

'You know a fair lot,' said Mrs MacAlister. 'What is it you don't know?'

'What kind of an accident it was,' replied Daisy. 'I want you to tell me what happened.'

The puzzlement intensified in Mrs MacAlister's pale grey, Highland eyes.

'What's your name?' she asked.

'Daisy,' said Daisy, impatiently.

'Well now, Daisy, I can answer your question, right enough. But what I'd like to know is how something that happened in 1746 can have got a wee lass like you into such a state. It was far more than two hundred years ago.'

'I know,' said Daisy exhaustedly. 'I'm sorry – I can't explain. It all seems so real. Please tell me – I'll be all right if I know.'

Mrs MacAlister sighed.

'It was a bitterly cold night,' she began, as one who had told the story many times. 'Lord Drummond was out with the Prince, you'll have heard, and the ladies were left at home with nobody worth talking about to look after them, MacAlister and Wishart likewise being out with the Laird. Now, a party of Redcoats that was trying to get back to England from Culloden happened to come by, and decided that Benalmond would be a good place to spend the night, with the Laird away, and the ladies not able to do much to stop them. So they wined and dined, and went to bed in the best chambers – though they did not molest the ladies, that much I will say for them. In the night, the stables caught fire – they do say one of the Redcoats had gone out to see to his horse that was lame, and dropped a light in the straw. Howsoever it was, the whole house burned down – folk said they could see the glow in the sky at Glasgow, thirty miles away. By a miracle, only one life was lost – the young stableman you mentioned, that the two ladies were so sweet on. And even he would have been saved, if he hadn't insisted on going back into the stable to bring out Miss Clementina's favourite horse.'

'Gib,' whispered Daisy. Then, gripping the sides of her

chair to steady herself, she made herself ask, 'What was his name, the young stableman?'

But she knew; she felt she had known for a long time. This was why poor Mick could not bring himself to contemplate the end of the story. Before her eyes, Daisy seemed to see again a tiny, cobweb-shrouded window, with four initials scratched in a corner. 'C. D. A. W.' – Charlotte Drummond and —

'He was a young Wishart,' Mrs MacAlister said. 'There have been Wisharts at Benalmond as long as there have been MacAlisters and Drummonds. It was sad, for his father was out with the Laird, and his mother had nine other wee mouths to feed.' She sighed again, and looked solemn. 'So you see —' she was about to continue, but Daisy interrupted her.

'I knew most of that,' she said, steadily. 'But now, if you don't mind, I'd like you to tell me what really happened.'

Mrs MacAlister stared at her, bristling just a little.

'What really happened?' she repeated, frowning. 'Haven't I just been telling you what really happened? It's in the history books.'

'I know it is. But that doesn't make it true,' said Daisy. 'There is another version, isn't there? I think you told it to Mr Briggs. In it, the Redcoat isn't the villain. It's someone else.'

This was taking a chance. Daisy only remembered in the vaguest way something that Mr Briggs had said about one of the young ladies doing the stableman in, the day he had told them about the ghost. But it was enough to get Mrs MacAlister going again.

'Ach, that!' she said impatiently. 'That's not history. It's gossip.'

'Even so, it might be true,' persisted Daisy. 'Please, Mrs MacAlister, I'd like to know.'

So Mrs MacAlister told her.

'It was said at the time – and it may, or may not be true, mind – that the Redcoat laddie got the blame for something he didn't do. There were rumours that on the same night, young Wishart and Miss Clementina Borde had arranged to meet in the hayloft, and that Miss Charlotte – who was maybe just a wee bit out of her mind with jealousy – got wind of it, and went looking for them with a lantern. It seems she had some idea that if she could catch them, and expose their love affair to her mother, her Ladyship would put a stop to it. Which was no doubt true. I don't think there was ever any suggestion that she had set the stable on fire deliberately, just that she had been careless with her lantern. Maybe it was fortunate that the Redcoats were there to blame, not that there was any proof of what happened, one way or the other. But you can understand why a family like the Drummonds preferred the story that got into the history books, can't you, Daisy?'

17
Fancy Dress

When Daisy came out of Mrs MacAlister's kitchen, a cool little breeze was agitating the branches of the trees, but beyond the loch the sun was descending steadily in a glory of crimson and gold. Daisy glanced down at her watch, and saw that its hands pointed out two minutes to nine. No sense in going back to the chalet; Bridget and her mother would certainly have left by now. Better, she thought, to go straight to the Tower, and find them there. She was amazed how calm and clear-headed she felt, and convinced that she alone could stay the hand of Fate. It was better to know than to fear, and now she knew what she would do. She would find Bridget, and come what might, she would stay close to her, never letting her out of her sight, till the Ball was over, and everyone safely in bed. Only twelve more hours, and they would have put Benalmond safely behind them, for ever. She, Daisy Bradbrook, would ensure that during this time, Bridget would have no opportunity for mischief. History would not repeat itself, for she would make sure that it had no chance to do so. Armed with this determination, she went down through the evergreen air of the wood, and made her way to the front of Benalmond Tower.

Even the sight of the preparations, the banks of flowers and the huge marquee, had not prepared Daisy for the magnificence of this occasion, which on Monday would feature prominently in the newspapers. Coloured lights twinkled among the trees, as expensive cars and battered Minis came bumping up the drive to drop off all manner of folk. The older ones were in ordinary evening dress, the younger in fancy dress costumes which were breath-taking in their colour and extravagance. A tube of toothpaste and a penguin got out of a Mercedes, a Pink Panther and Little Bo-Peep got out of a Rolls Royce. Then a kilted sheep and a gorilla came along in a battered Ford. It seemed that everyone on the estate who had not been invited had come along to watch; each new arrival was greeted by a burst of good-natured laughter, and some sporadic applause. Feeling very little and lonely, Daisy joined the queue of guests which was moving very slowly towards the entrance. The sheep said, 'Good evening,' and the gorilla made gorilla noises. Daisy suspected that the gorilla had already had a good deal to drink. But she did not pay much attention. Light shone from the open door, and beyond a babble of competing voices she could hear music, an orchestra playing those eighteenth century tunes which for the rest of her days would send a shiver running down her spine. Now she was on the doorstep, with the heavy scent of freesias and gardenias all around her; now, as she stepped over the threshold, she realised why everyone was moving so slowly. There was a reception line, like one at a wedding. Mick and Wendy, and a smiling middle-aged couple who must be Mick's father and mother, were welcoming the guests one by one, before passing them on to Winnie, Angus and Clementina. Their job, apparently, was to see that they all had glasses of wine, and someone to talk to.

Daisy shook hands politely with Lord and Lady Drummond, but she could not take her eyes for more than a second from the group from the stables. With a painful leaping of her heart, she understood why

Clementina, in parting, had laughed so provokingly at Bridget.

For they were all in eighteenth century costume – not copied from a book and put together on a sewing-machine from modern materials, but genuine, heirloom clothes such as Daisy had never seen outside a museum. Mick was most splendid in brown velvet breeches and a coat of rose-pink brocade. He had black buckled shoes and white silk stockings, and lace at his throat and wrists. Angus was more soberly dressed in black and dull green, although he had a fine gold-embroidered waistcoat. The girls – including Clementina, no doubt by Angus's insistence – were dressed in softly coloured silks and satins, with ruffles of creamy lace on their sleeves and around the low, square-cut necks of their gowns. The sheer, unexpected beauty of their clothes distanced this group from all the spacemen and wizards and harlequins who were their guests. Bathed in the ancient light of many candles, they stood like strangers in that crowded room.

But then Daisy found her hand in Mick's, warm and reassuring, and could not help a glow of pleasure as he bent down and kissed her lightly on the cheek.

'Thanks for that super card you sent me,' he said. 'Do you like my togs?'

'Fantastic,' said Daisy sincerely.

'Just pray that my breeks don't give way,' whispered Mick, and Daisy was swallowed up in the crowd, clutching a glass of champagne and looking frantically for Bridget.

Eventually, by dint of much squeezing and wriggling, she located her and her mother on the far side of the room. Bridget, in her pretty dress which, until now, had seemed so perfectly to mirror the eighteenth century, was looking sulky, and Daisy did not blame her. Mrs Graham, who always found someone to talk to, was being boisterous with the gorilla. The champagne had already brought a sparkle to her blue eyes, and she waved happily to Daisy.

'Coo-ee! I've just met this charming gorilla,' she called. 'He went to University near Reading.'

'Oxford, actually,' said the gorilla.

Daisy went and stood beside Bridget, who moved away impatiently. Daisy went after her, and was told rudely to push off. It was going to prove very difficult to keep close to Bridget for any length of time. Perhaps, Daisy thought, she should try instead to keep her in sight from a distance. But even this proved almost impossible, and she felt panic rising.

Once everyone was assembled, there were speeches, first from Lord Drummond, telling everyone what a marvellous son Mick was, then from Mick, returning the compliment to his Mum and Dad. Then there was an unscheduled speech from the gorilla, cut short by the imperious little granny whom he apparently shared with Mick.

'Do be quiet, Douglas. Who wants to listen to you?'

Much applause then, as the gorilla embraced his granny, and everyone began to move into the side rooms for supper.

Daisy helped herself to a tiny portion of cold salmon mousse and salad from a buffet groaning under its burden of good things to eat. She had never felt less hungry. By placing herself beside the narrow doorway, she could make sure that Bridget would not go out without passing her. She noticed that Bridget had met one of the boys who had come to the three-day camp, and was chatting to him quite vivaciously. This was good, Daisy thought grimly, as she forced herself to swallow a slice of tomato. Having a partner she liked just might divert Bridget from whatever it was she had in mind. When supper was over, she followed them, at a distance, out to the marquee where the dancing was to be held, and tried to keep them in her view. She managed too, although it was difficult in the merry throng which now came surging out of the supper rooms, to take up their positions around the wooden dance floor in the marquee.

There were two bands, at one end a kilted Scottish country dance band, and at the other a sequinned pop group called The Bears. Daisy had not expected to be asked to dance much, but as soon as the first order had been given, 'My Lords and Gentlemen, pray take your partners for "The Dashing White Sergeant",' the tube of toothpaste and the sheep came rushing over and drew her into the dance. After that, keeping an eye on Bridget became a nightmare, as Daisy was chosen every time; boys she had met at the Trekking Centre asked her, strangers asked her – it would have been the best night of her life, she reflected bitterly, had it not been for Clementina Rattray and Bridget Graham.

Every so often, in the set reels, she met Mick, dancing with his mother, or his granny, or Mrs Graham. He would roll his eyes at her, and wink, and point surreptitiously to his breeches. Angus, after dancing once with Lady Drummond and once with Wendy, danced only with Clementina. It seemed to Daisy that they looked equally haggard and unhappy; they watched each other with unswerving intensity, but Daisy did not see either of them smile, once.

It was getting on for midnight when Mrs Graham, bright red in the face and panting with exertion, passed Daisy and said, 'That's enough for an old woman, I think. I don't want to cause a sensation by having a heart attack in the middle of the floor, so I'm off now. See you in the morning. Night-night.'

Daisy said good-night. She was watching Mrs Graham making her exit, waving and bowing and thoroughly enjoying herself, when she saw Angus and

Clementina, hand in hand, slip out through the looped-up canvas ahead of her. In a fright, Daisy looked round for Bridget, and sure enough, there she was, breaking away from her partner and pushing her way round the perimeter of the floor. Daisy pushed too, and caught up with her in the doorway; not caring now who saw them, she grabbed Bridget by the arm.

'Where are you going?' she demanded, in a high voice that did not seem to be her own.

Furiously, Bridget shook her off. 'Mind your own business,' she hissed. 'What has it got to do with you where I go? Get out of the way!'

She tried to push past, but Daisy, beside herself with anxiety, again caught her by the sleeve.

'Biddy, don't,' she pleaded. 'You don't know what you're doing. Come back and dance, please. It's pitch dark in the stables – you'll never find them. Forget it, for your own sake!'

Bridget stared at her, as if she had not the remotest idea what she was talking about. Then an extraordinary expression, compounded of anger, incredulity and – could it possibly be amusement? – came across her face.

'Stables?' she said. 'That's an idea. Thanks.'

And giving Daisy a spiteful push, she ran away from her across the gravel.

Daisy made to follow, but at that instant, the Fate which she had thought to outwit took over. A large hand was laid gently on her shoulder, and a voice she loved said in her ear, 'Our dance, Miss Bradbrook, if I may have the pleasure.' And drawing her arm politely through his own, Mick led her away to the top of the first set, to dance the Eightsome Reel.

At any other time, to have danced with Mick Drummond would have been sheer delight to Daisy. Now, it was sheer misery. They danced the reel twice, and she had to nod and smile and set to partners, while in her head a silent scream went on, and on, and on. And when at last the dance was over, and Mick had escorted her from the floor, still she could not get away, because Mick wanted to introduce her to his parents, who were nice, and asked her about herself, and said they hoped she would come and see them at Balquhidder one day. Then Wendy came to say goodbye, and to tell her how much she looked forward to meeting her again in October, in Aberdeen. It would all have been so heart-warming and astonishing, had she not been so desperate to be gone.

By the time she was free, her watch told her it was five to one. There was no point in trying to find Bridget now, she knew. If she had gone to the stables, that had been nearly an hour ago, and it was most unlikely that she was still there. And anyway, outside the magical, lamp-lit circle of the Tower in its best dress, the night was impenetrably dark. There was no moon, and a chilly breeze was blowing itself into a wind over the invisible surface of the loch. Feeling cold and very weary, Daisy decided that she might as well go home.

18
Night

Never again, in all her life, would Daisy experience a moment of such perfect relief as she did when she pushed open the door of the bedroom, and saw, by the light on the stair behind her, Clementina and Bridget under their duvets, apparently asleep. She undressed silently, and went into the bathroom, where she cleaned her teeth, laughing and crying at the same time. What a fool she had been to lose control of her common sense, to let her imagination get the better of her. It all seemed so obvious now. Angus and Clementina, not in a party mood, had left early. Angus had brought Clementina back to the chalet, and gone off to his own bed. Bridget had realised the foolishness of trying to find anyone in the pitch darkness behind the Tower, and had come home instead. Daisy felt one sharp pang of regret, when she remembered how she had spoiled a lovely evening for herself, but most of all there was just the wonderful sense of a burden lifted away. She switched off the light, slipped into bed, and fell immediately into a deep, untroubled sleep.

Daisy could not have said which it was that woke her, the wildly flickering light which engulfed the whole house, or the noise of banging doors and excited voices as their neighbours left their chalets and pounded past theirs along the path to the Tower. Clementina and Bridget were up, and already pulling on their clothes;

with violently thudding heart Daisy sat up, and reached for her jersey. She could hear Mrs Graham blundering around in the room next door, but she was dressed before her, and running out into the wood where birds were rising from their roosts with hysterical cries, and the spaces between the branches were coloured an evil, sullen maroon. In front of Daisy as she ran was the terrible, unsteady glow of a great fire, lighting up trees and buildings, reflecting bloodily in the windows of the holiday homes. It seemed that everyone on the estate was moving in the same direction, and Daisy was swept along with them. But when she stumbled up to the fence that bounded the paddock, where they had first met Angus, she was stopped by a man she did not know.

'Stay where you are, lass,' he said authoritatively. 'No one's to go any nearer. There's nothing anybody can do.'

Sobbing for breath, Daisy leaned against the fence, and forced herself to look at the appalling scene before her.

The ranch house, the harness room and the row of loose boxes along the rear wall of the Tower were all on fire. Flames licked brilliantly around their walls, and burst triumphantly through their roofs, like sprays of golden flowers. The burning air was full of noises, voices calling, horses whinnying in terror, the roar and wicked crackle of the flames. As her eyes focused, Daisy saw in the rosy light Mick and Angus and Jeff the groom, leading out the ponies, shying and kicking, with cloths over their eyes, and turning them loose at the far end of the paddock. Beyond them, a chain of helpers had formed. Buckets of water were being passed rhythmically from hand to hand. It was like using a fire extinguisher to put out Vesuvius.

Daisy heard her own voice moaning, 'Oh, Tam, Tam,' and then Bridget's voice behind her, saying quite calmly, 'It's all right. Don't worry – he's out. So are Coxy and Tinker.'

Daisy turned, and saw Bridget, with Mrs Graham and Clementina, standing just behind her. Mrs Graham's face looked stupid with disbelief; Daisy could not bear to look at Clementina's. She looked away, and saw Mick and Angus standing in the paddock, wiping their foreheads on their sleeves, and staring at each other in despair. Then somebody shouted, 'Stand away, lads! It's too late!' and almost in the same instant, Daisy heard Clementina's voice, shrill and wild above the rest.

'Gib! Gib! Oh, Angus, where's Gib?'

Angus turned towards her, silhouetted black against the fearful light. Then, before Mick could stop him, he sprinted back towards the burning stable, and disappeared inside. A shuddering sigh went up from the onlookers. Then the roof fell in. With an exultant roar the flames leaped skywards, and the sparks were like golden stars.

And now Daisy saw something very strange. Afterwards, she would always know that she really had seen it, because Mick, who did not believe in ghosts, told her that he had seen it too. Just as Clementina fell fainting into Mrs Graham's arms, and no one else seemed able to move at all, a young man in a white shirt and dark breeches came walking out of the fire. He was leading a dark horse, which walked quietly and confidently at his side. When they got clear of the burning buildings, they paused, and after the young man had patted the horse's nose, and talked to him a little, he leaped lightly up on to his back. Then, looking neither to right nor to left, he rode silently through the paddock, and took the bridle-path into the wood.

Postscript:
Canadian Spring

Ten years had passed. Ten years, since that night of desolation, with its terrible aftermath of guilt and anger and sense of loss. Ten years which, inevitably, had wiped away the worst of the anger and grief, but, in Daisy, had left the feeling of guilt intact. Till now.

Now it was April, in Canada. The snow had gone, there was warmth in the sun, and Mick and Wendy had come to stay. Daisy had wondered how it would be; for years they had been so close. All through Wendy's University years, they had all three been firm friends, despite the gap in their ages, and Daisy had been a bridesmaid at Mick and Wendy's wedding. For the last three years, however, they had not met at all. Before their arrival, Daisy had felt absurdly shy, and she had wondered – with memories of Benalmond giving her no rest – whether she really wanted to meet them again.

But when she had seen them walking across the tarmac at the airport, unchanged, except that Mick was a little heavier, a little more weather-beaten, she had known in an instant how ridiculous such thoughts had been. She had waved, and run to hug them at the barrier, and they had started talking as if they had parted only yesterday.

Of course, after that, the week had flown by in a rush of sightseeing and eating and drinking and laughing and talking. Wendy, who so far had produced only daughters, was delighted with Daisy's nine-month-old twin boys, and swore that she would steal one of them when she went home. Somehow, the Benalmond episode was never mentioned; Mick had abandoned his plans for a riding establishment there soon after the fire; he had bought a farm beyond Strathyre, where he now bred racehorses. Not until the last evening, when Rodney had gone out because he was on night duty at the hospital, and the three old friends were sitting round the kitchen table with their coffee, did Wendy say, 'I mustn't forget to tell you, Daisy. Last month, we met Clementina Rattray.'

Daisy was aware that they were both watching her, wondering how she would react to this statement. Clementina Rattray's was not a name which had ever been mentioned much among them. But if – as Mick said – Daisy had hardly changed at all in appearance between the ages of thirteen and twenty-three, she had at least learned to guard her expression. So, although her stomach was lurching uncomfortably, she did manage to raise her eyebrows, and say calmly, 'Good heavens, did you really? After all this time? How did that come about?'

She saw Mick, who did not control his features particularly well, relax, and look relieved.

'It was after a concert in Edinburgh,' he told her. 'A gala affair, in aid of some kids' charity of which my mamma is President – so we all had to turn out, like it or not. Clementina Rattray was the guest soloist – apparently she's a very celebrated lady these days – and afterwards we met her at a bun fight.'

Daisy, who more than once had turned off the television in a fright, because Clementina Rattray was billed to appear, could not help finding all this fascinating.

'What was she like?' she asked.

Mick was silent, and it was Wendy who answered.

'Nice,' she said. 'Still very handsome, but quiet, and not at all grand. She told us that she is going to be married in June – to her violin teacher, Walter Lauenstein. He was at the party too. He must be twenty years older than she is, but he seemed very kind, and protective. I think they'll be happy together.'

Daisy said she was glad. She paused for a moment, then added, 'I used to worry – in case she would never marry at all. She really did love Angus, you know.'

'Ten years is long enough to be loyal,' said Mick gruffly.

'She asked about you,' Wendy went on. 'I told her that you were married, and about the twins. She seemed amused, but of course she hasn't seen you since you were a kid. Anyway, she said I was to give you her love, and tell you she's sorry.'

'Sorry?' repeated Daisy, surprised. 'Sorry for what?'

'Sorry for not being nicer to you. She said she thought you would understand that unhappiness can make people nasty when they don't want to be.'

Daisy nodded.

'It was nice of her to remember,' she said.

There was silence in the kitchen for a while, broken only by the ticking of the clock on the wall, and the hum of the refrigerator. Daisy got up and made another jug of coffee. When she sat down again, she made herself ask, 'Wendy – did Clementina mention Bridget?'

'No,' Wendy said. 'Why? Should she have?'

'Oh, I don't know. I just wondered,' replied Daisy. 'They hated each other so much. I'd have thought Bridget would be nearer the surface of her memory than I would, to tell you the truth.'

'I see. Do you ever hear news of Bridget these days?' Wendy enquired.

Daisy shook her head.

'I haven't heard anything for years,' she said. 'Not

long – afterwards, you know, she and her mother went to live in Reading. But I don't think things could have worked out for them there, because the following summer they went to Australia, to visit Bridget's aunts, and decided to stay. I had a postcard from Bridget, telling me what a super place Melbourne was, and how awful it was for me to be stuck in a dump like Aberdeen – which was exactly what she said when she went to Reading. But after that, I never heard from her again.'

Mick pushed back his chair, stretched out his long legs, and entered the conversation abruptly.

'It's strange,' he said. 'I know there was no proof, but I've always suspected that girl was at the stables on the night of the fire. I don't know why I should think so, and I'm aware that I may be doing her a terrible injustice, but – I've always wondered, and I reckon I always will.'

'There's no reason to believe that, my love,' Wendy reproved him, gently.

Now a struggle began in Daisy which threatened to tear her apart. For ten years she had feared this moment, and now it was upon her, the moment in which a choice must be made. She must choose either to stay silent, and carry her burden of knowledge alone for ever, or to tell these dear friends everything, and risk their shocked disapproval, but be rid at last of the pain and strain of being the only one who knew. She looked from Mick's brown, ugly, kindly face to Wendy's honest, sensible one, and made up her mind.

Taking a deep breath, she said flatly, 'You needn't wonder any longer, Mick. She did go to the stables that night. I know she did.'

Two pairs of eyes were turned upon her, alert and fascinated.

'How do you know?' Mick asked.

It was too late to go back now, even if she had wanted to.

Daisy said, 'In the morning – when we were doing our last-minute packing – I saw the shoes she had been wearing at the Ball. They were covered with mud, and bits of straw. I saw her wrapping them up in newspaper, when she thought nobody was watching, and burying them away down at the bottom of her suitcase. And there was another thing. There was a paraffin lantern, that used to hang on a hook at the back door of the chalet – for power cuts, I suppose. Well – it had been moved, into the garage. I reckon that after she left the Tower, about midnight, she went back to the chalet, fetched the lantern, and went to the stables. She must just have missed Angus and Clementina, who – I think – went straight home. I suppose that after Bridget had been to the stables, and realised they weren't there after all, she came back and went to bed. That would explain why she and Clementina were both there when I got in at one o'clock – having danced with you, Mick, and talked a bit to your Mum and Dad.'

Mick was looking stunned. He emitted one of the low whistles by which he expressed himself when he was at a loss for words.

It was Wendy who said, gently as ever, 'Daisy love – when the police came, and questioned everyone – didn't it occur to you that perhaps you ought to tell them all this?'

'Yes, yes!' cried Daisy, almost violently. 'Of course it did. Don't you see – I've been tortured for ten years, not knowing whether I did right or wrong. But it seemed right then, and – yes, whatever anyone else thinks, it seems right now. It wasn't only that she didn't set the stable on fire on purpose – there's more to it than that.'

Mick and Wendy looked at each other, in perturbation. But then Mick leaned towards Daisy across the table, and said, 'Tell us, please. It will help us – and I can only think it will also help you.'

'Yes,' Daisy agreed. She took a moment or two to put what she wanted to say in order, then she went on. 'I felt – that Bridget was not to blame. I know she was a ghastly kid, but if you believe – as I do – that the events of that summer were a weird replay of events that had happened already, more than two hundred years before, Bridget wasn't responsible for her part in them. In some way which we will never begin to understand, the coming together of Clementina and the past of Benalmond set the train of happenings in motion, but, after that had happened – is it not true that the people involved were just like actors in a play which they didn't even know was being performed? They were victims of an uncanny process, and simply couldn't help themselves. If Bridget Graham was cast in the role of Charlotte Drummond, that was her doom – she was as much a victim as Angus and Clementina, and even that poor horse, Billy.'

Mick nodded his head slowly.

'You mean,' he said seriously, 'that Bridget had no free will in the matter?'

'Yes, I do,' said Daisy. 'In fact, I'm sure of it. You see, it wasn't just that Bridget wanted Angus, and was jealous of Clementina, like Charlotte Drummond long ago. She even *thought* the same way as Charlotte Drummond. Mrs MacAlister told me that Charlotte Drummond believed that if she could expose Clementina Borde's love affair with the stableman, Lady Arabella would put a stop to it. Well, fair enough. What's ridiculous is that Bridget thought the same thing. Before the Ball, she said to me, "Before tomorrow, I'm going to make sure that *Mother* and everyone else knows what a hypocrite she really is." Well, I mean – think of it. Mrs Graham! She wouldn't have cared tuppence what

Clementina was doing at the stables, just as long as she wasn't bothered. If she had been – herself, Bridget would have known that perfectly well.'

'And that was why you didn't tell the Police, or anybody?' asked Wendy.

'Yes. I couldn't see why Bridget's life should be spoiled – and it would have been spoiled – because of something for which she had no real responsibility.' She stopped for a moment, wondering whether she ought to go on. Mick and Wendy were looking astonished, but she could see neither disapproval nor hostility in their eyes. Anyway, it made no odds. She had to tell the rest now. If she did, she would be able to sleep tonight.

'Besides,' she continued slowly, 'there was something else. Something which made it my fault as much as hers. No, please, don't contradict me, Mick – just let me tell you. It was I who told Bridget that Angus and Clementina might be at the stables. I thought she knew, but afterwards, I realised that she didn't. When she went out of the marquee, and I went after her to try to stop her following Angus and Clementina, I was in an awful tizzy, and I said, "It will be pitch dark in the stables!" She looked at me in such a funny way, and said, "The stables? That's a good idea. Thanks." God forgive me, until that minute I don't think going there had ever occurred to her.'

Daisy dropped her head into her hands, and there was another little silence, broken only by the humdrum, normal, household sounds.

Eventually, Mick said, 'So you were a victim too, little one. I wonder who your counterpart was in the eighteenth century?'

Daisy raised her eyes, and stared at him.

'I hadn't thought of that,' she said. 'Then – you're not angry? You don't think I did wrong?'

'No. You did right,' said Mick stoutly. 'Didn't she, Wendy?'

'Without a shred of doubt,' Wendy agreed.

Upstairs, a baby cried.

'That's Michael,' said Daisy. 'I had better go up.'

She rose from the table, pushing her hair back from her face, and went out into the hall. But before she had time to switch on the light, the wailing upstairs trailed off into a chuckle, and the child slept again. Daisy turned to go back into the kitchen, but ran up against Mick, who had followed her out into the hall. He sat down on the bottom step of the stair, and drew her down beside him.

'There's something I want to tell you,' he said quietly. 'Something that's just between you and me. You remember, on the night Angus died, the young man we saw riding in the paddock, on a dark horse? Nobody else saw them – only us two.'

Daisy found his hand in the darkness, and gave it a squeeze.

'Yes,' she said.

'It was Angus, Daisy. I've seen him again, three times – twice at Balquhidder, and once in a wood above Strathyre. I've never been close to him, and I never see him for more than a few seconds – but each time I've been overcome by the most wonderful feeling of peace, and well-being. I don't think you need to feel guilty about anything that happened. It's all history now.'